TRY TO LOVE THE QUESTIONS

SKILLS FOR SCHOLARS

Try to Love the Questions: From Debate to Dialogue in Classrooms and Life, Lara Hope Schwartz

The Elements of Visual Grammar: A Designer's Guide for Writers, Scholars, and Professionals, Angela Riechers

Writing with Pleasure, Helen Sword

The Secret Syllabus: A Guide to the Unwritten Rules of College Success, Jay Phelan and Terry Burnham

The Economist's Craft: An Introduction to Research, Publishing, and Professional Development, Michael S. Weisbach

How to Think like Shakespeare: Lessons from a Renaissance Education, Scott Newstok

The Book Proposal Book: A Guide for Scholarly Authors, Laura Portwood-Stacer

The Princeton Guide to Historical Research, Zachary M. Schrag

You Are What You Read: A Practical Guide to Reading Well, Robert DiYanni

Super Courses: The Future of Teaching and Learning, Ken Bain

Syllabus: The Remarkable, Unremarkable Document That Changes Everything, William Germano and Kit Nicholls

Leaving Academia: A Practical Guide, Christopher L. Caterine

A Field Guide to Grad School: Uncovering the Hidden Curriculum, Jessica McCrory Calarco

The Craft of College Teaching: A Practical Guide, Robert DiYanni and Anton Borst

Will This Be on the Test?, Dana T. Johnson and Jennifer E. Price

Try to Love the Questions

FROM DEBATE TO DIALOGUE IN CLASSROOMS AND LIFE

LARA HOPE SCHWARTZ

PRINCETON UNIVERSITY PRESS
PRINCETON & OXFORD

Published by Princeton University Press
41 William Street, Princeton, New Jersey 08540
99 Banbury Road, Oxford OX2 6JX

press.princeton.edu

Library of Congress Cataloging-in-Publication Data

Names: Schwartz, Lara Hope, author.
Title: Try to love the questions : from debate to dialogue in classrooms and life / Lara Hope Schwartz.
Description: Princeton ; Oxford : Princeton University Press, [2024] | Series: Skills for scholars | Includes bibliographical references and index.
Identifiers: LCCN 2023041355 (print) | LCCN 2023041356 (ebook) | ISBN 9780691239996 (hbk. : acid-free paper) | ISBN 9780691240008 (pbk. : acid-free paper) | ISBN 9780691240015 (e-book)
Subjects: LCSH: Communication in education. | Interpersonal communication. | Intercultural communication. | Rhetoric—Study and teaching (Higher) | Debates and debating—Study and teaching (Higher) | Self-realization. | BISAC: EDUCATION / Schools / Levels / Higher | EDUCATION / Teaching / General
Classification: LCC LB1033.5 .S366 2024 (print) | LCC LB1033.5 (ebook) | DDC 371.102/2—dc23/eng/20230919
LC record available at https://lccn.loc.gov/2023041355
LC ebook record available at https://lccn.loc.gov/2023041356

British Library Cataloging-in-Publication Data is available

Editorial: Matt Rohal and Alena Chekanov
Production Editorial: Kathleen Cioffi
Cover Design: Heather Hansen
Production: Erin Suydam
Publicity: Alyssa Sanford and Kathryn Stevens
Copyeditor: Anne Sanow

This book has been composed in Arno

Printed on acid-free paper. ∞

Printed in the United States of America

10 9 8 7 6 5 4 3 2 1

In memory of Barbra Jane Klubes,
who taught me the immense power of listening.

And for Philip Klubes, who continues to
show me how to lovingly disagree.

You are so young, so much before all beginning, and I would like to beg you, dear Sir, as well as I can, to have patience with everything unresolved in your heart and to try to love the questions themselves as if they were locked rooms or books written in a very foreign language. Don't search for the answers, which could not be given to you now, because you would not be able to live them. And the point is, to live everything. Live the questions now. Perhaps then, someday far in the future, you will gradually, without even noticing it, live your way into the answer.

—RAINER MARIA RILKE, *LETTERS TO A YOUNG POET*

CONTENTS

PROLOGUE

On Trying

MUCH HAS BEEN written about whether colleges must choose between rigorous inquiry and preserving free expression on the one hand, and prioritizing kindness and inclusivity on the other. As someone who loved college, and who decided to go back and teach when I rediscovered that love deep into my career as a lawyer, I've been dismayed by the pessimism in much of this writing. If you are reading this book because you are starting college soon and you're worried that college will be a place for raised voices and closed minds, let me take a moment to reassure you now: the picture of college discourse I find in the opinion pages looks nothing like any classroom I know.

It seems to me that the pessimistic view of higher education—and most particularly of students—misses the point. I am still humbled when I consider my students' extraordinarily optimistic act of committing themselves to higher education. From where I stand, the protests, the friction, and the institutional infighting over how best to fulfill our missions and protect our communities are not signs of sickness. They are signs that we are trying. Sometimes, our efforts work well. I've facilitated hundreds of class meetings about civil rights and liberties, constitutional law, politics, criminal justice, activism, advocacy, and democracy. The best ones had a certain electricity, and the 75-minute class periods felt unforgivably short. Many of the details of these successful conversations are not memorable now, but that unique classroom feeling, the special something about being in conversation together, is always vivid to me.

Some conversations are memorable for having been less successful, usually because I wasn't great at making the material resonate for the students yet. (I fear I'll still be trying to figure out how to structure an exciting lesson on campaign finance at my retirement party.) And there have been times when hard words or tense silence prevailed for what felt like too long. I don't regret those class sessions nearly as much as I would regret avoiding the complex, difficult, often painful material that makes up my courses on law and politics. If you want to have vibrant, challenging conversations about things that matter, you can find them in my classroom and in thousands of college classrooms across this country.

The truth is that colleges and universities try to do something that almost nobody else does. Colleges bring together people from urban, rural, and suburban areas across the country and around the world, from varying household types, identities, socioeconomic classes, races, and points of view, building classrooms and communities where all these people are in conversation with one another. Colleges bring people together in conversation like nowhere else.

Most of us in the twenty-first-century Not-So-United States of America live in communities where conversation across differences is harder to come by. Many of our elders live in separate communities. Even in racially diverse cities, neighborhoods are sorted by income and often by race. Progressive people who purport to be supporters of diversity and inclusiveness are often some of the strongest defenders of exclusionary zoning regulations. Many children attend schools that are racially and economically homogeneous, reflecting their communities. And if we look at our electoral maps, an increasing number of us live in hyperpolarized, hyperpartisan counties, census tracts, and towns where one party or the other predominates. Media consumption reveals and reinforces our separation.

But in colleges and universities, we gather to be in conversation with one another. We *try* to have communities where we are not combatants, but colleagues. And although the range of our identities, viewpoints, and educational goals are as wide as the world, our shared identity as scholars and learners—people who try to understand things better, and who study mechanisms for better understanding—binds college communities in a way that ought to be a model for life beyond college.

What I have seen in college classrooms gives me hope for humanity. Back-to-school is a magical time for me because of the wild, challenging, often hard conversations that unfold in my courses on law and government. To come to college and enter these conversations is brave, and participating in them can be hard. As scholars and students, we *live* the questions, and develop the bravery to resist the pull of unwarranted certainty.

Even as I write this, people disagree passionately, and in good faith, about whether higher education is as I've described.

This book does not purport to serve as a rebuttal to that point of view. In fact, I think it would be a great tool to enable students to engage deeply with that disagreement. In my experience, college students are capable of thoughtful dialogue on this and many other important topics.

This book is titled "Try to Love the Questions," not simply "Love the Questions," because what I'm asking of you is hard. It is hard to abandon one's preconceived ideas. It is hard to let down our defensiveness. It is hard to start from "I don't know" and build toward informed and generous opinions. We are trying, and those of us who *try* should know to expect imperfection. We do not expect to have all the answers or to be very skilled in our early attempts. We never expect the learning process to be over.

It is hard to start our education with great aspirations and crash into the reality that colleges and universities are populated by mere humans, with all our flaws and misconceptions and even cruelty. It can be hard to keep loving the pursuit of education in disturbing times that are frequently called "extraordinary."

It is hard, but we are trying, with all the messiness, friction, and painstaking progress that entails.

This book is for those who are interested in trying.

TRY TO LOVE THE QUESTIONS

1

Think If You Should

PARADIGM SHIFTS ON CAMPUS DISCOURSE

If there is a bedrock principle underlying the First Amendment, it is that the government may not prohibit the expression of an idea simply because society finds the idea itself offensive or disagreeable.

—*TEXAS V. JOHNSON*, 491 U.S. 397 (1989)

Your scientists were so preoccupied with whether or not they could that they didn't stop to think if they should.

—*JURASSIC PARK* (1993)

THE QUOTATIONS ABOVE represent two central aspects of this book's subject matter: the skill of good-faith dialogue. The first is from *Texas v. Johnson*, a Supreme Court decision that struck down a criminal ban on flag desecration.[1] Mr. Johnson,

1. *Texas v. Johnson*, 491 U.S. 397 (1989).

who had burned a US flag outside of the Republican National Convention as a form of protest, was prosecuted under a law that banned burning flags. The Court ruled that the Texas flag desecration law (which permitted people to burn flags in order to dispose of them, as required by military protocol, but not in protest, as Johnson had)[2] violated the First Amendment right to freedom of speech. The fact that the expression was distasteful to others, the Court concluded, did not entitle the state of Texas to outlaw it.

This is the essence of expressive freedom (what is often shorthanded as "free speech"): authorities may not pick and choose which speech to censor or punish based on viewpoint. And we, the people, have the freedom to express ourselves regardless of whether our ideas are popular or palatable.

The second quotation is from the 1993 movie *Jurassic Park*, in which a wealthy businessman hires scientists to develop living dinosaurs from preserved genetic material and display them in an amusement park. (Spoiler alert: it does not go well.) A mathematician hired as a consultant—after the fateful decision to reproduce prehistoric carnivores was made—observes that the scientists were so focused on what they could do, that they made a huge (and deadly) error regarding what they should do.

This quote captures what our First Amendment does not—the complex and fascinating question of how we *should* use our freedom. In this book, I propose that learning and practicing

2. Katie Lange, "How to Properly Dispose of Worn-Out U.S. Flags," US Department of Defense, June 11, 2020, https://www.defense.gov/News/Feature-Stories/story/article/2206946/how-to-properly-dispose-of-worn-out-us-flags/.

good-faith dialogue is a better use of that freedom than debating, trolling, or retreating to the comfort of untested certainty. Good-faith dialogue encompasses far more than just the freedom to speak—and yet it cannot flourish without that freedom.

Academic dialogue requires both freedom and compassion to thrive. It has become conventional wisdom that these two priorities are in tension and that administrators tasked with promoting equity and inclusion are at odds with faculty, students, or politicians concerned about preserving free inquiry. But what if equity—including communicating and listening with care—was not a limitation on freedom, but rather a skill that opens doors to deeper understanding? In my experience, people have deeper, more meaningful, rigorous, and productive conversations once we understand that speaking and listening across differences is a core skill, much like writing, research, or keeping a budget.

This is the shift in thinking I ask of my students and fellow educators and that I will share with you. Dialogue is a skill that can and must be taught and practiced in an atmosphere where participants enjoy liberty, embrace personal responsibility and accountability, accept the possibility that we could be wrong, and commit to try again tomorrow where we fall short today.

Why Isn't It Enough to Learn about "Free Speech"?

This book concerns itself with expression: the act of intentionally conveying meaning through speech, actions, art, or some combination of these. Dialogue, including good-faith dialogue, involves expression, as well as (importantly) listening and learning. Asking questions, reading assigned materials, conducting research, and listening to the people around us are all critical components of the learning process. But what most of us call "class participation" isn't the subject of many books. In my experience, teachers and students don't talk enough about what good class participation entails. In these pages, I will explore many communicative elements of this work, including reading, listening, formulating questions, communicating ideas orally and in writing, deploying evidence with precision, accepting feedback, and synthesizing and comparing concepts and ideas.

When we talk about "free speech," we really mean the broader category of expression and expressive conduct (such as saluting a flag or kneeling during the national anthem). Many conversations about expression in the United States today concern themselves mostly with the question of whether anyone—for example the government, a school, or a corporation—may punish expression or stop it from happening at all. That is an important question, and I will introduce you to the rules (such as laws against harassment) and norms (such as the practice of avoiding profanity) that apply to many kinds of speech and expressive conduct. To understand matters of particular interest to higher education communities (such as invited speakers, hateful speech, student protests, and misinformation) we must explore these rules and norms.

But communication is about far more than rules. To understand this, consider one way you express yourself: clothing. When you get dressed, you probably follow certain rules, such as "no shirt, no shoes, no service." You also follow certain practices we call norms. Casual clothes for a movie theater but slightly nicer clothes for a date, and more formal clothes for a debate tournament or job interview. The government did not create these norms but failing to follow them can have real consequences.

Your clothing choices often reflect how you want to present yourself and what you want to express. Maybe you wear a t-shirt with your favorite band's name on it to show what kind of art you enjoy. You might dress particularly carefully for a job interview to convey that you will fit in with the organization and that you take the opportunity and the occasion seriously.

A school's dress code would not give a new student any idea of how students dress in their community, nor how they can show their own personal style. If you have ever moved to a new community or school, you might have felt curious or even anxious about these unwritten norms and looked to other community members for guidance. Maybe your clothing choices made for an awkward first day at school or at an internship—overdressed, underdressed, or simply out of place.

Just as the dress code can't teach us how to fit in (or stand out), the rules governing speech and expression don't tell us how to become successful learners, effective communicators, responsible community members, or supportive friends. Copyright law says we may not pass off Beyoncé's *Renaissance* as our own—but it doesn't teach us to write songs. The First Amendment prevents the governor from censoring her challenger's political ad, but it doesn't help us determine whether claims in the ad are true. There are laws against assault and harassment but there is no law on how to be kind. That is why I often remind students that the First Amendment is only a limitation on government—not a blueprint for how to live.

Being a skilled and effective communicator means more than understanding what we are free to say. It means reflecting on what we want to communicate and why; our strengths and challenges as listeners, including listening with curiosity; becoming comfortable with questions and developing research skills to seek answers; learning how to convey our thoughts in clear and understandable ways; and receiving and responding to feedback with gratitude.

What's So Special about Good-Faith Dialogue?

College courses (and civic life) require us to practice a form of listening, speaking, and questioning that we might not have practiced much before. As you will learn in Chapter 3 of this book, students in K-12 schools in the United States have limited freedom of expression compared to college students or other adults. If you arrive at college without much practice discussing complex issues, solving challenging problems in collaboration with others, or expressing disagreement with peers or authority figures, you're not alone.

Much of the dialogue outside of academic spaces doesn't provide a great model for what we try to do in college or for when we are trying to solve problems in the public interest. By the time we reach college, most of us have been exposed to political campaigns in which candidates representing the major political parties make their case to voters. Political campaigns expose us to conflict and disagreement (also features of academic and civic dialogue), but they are fundamentally different from what we do in classes. Campaigns generally present binary possibilities. You may vote for candidate A or B, red or blue. In academic dialogue, by contrast, there are infinite answers to the questions we explore. While a campaign asks "Who is the better choice?" in an academic dialogue, we ask "How might we better understand a problem, and what would we need to know in order to address it?"

I believe that the kind of dialogue we practice in our college classrooms is a good model for civic engagement: working collaboratively to address common problems and create practicable solutions. This is different from partisan campaigning, where the goal is not solely to solve a substantive problem, but to get a majority of voters to select one candidate (even as many candidates run for office with the objective of solving a specific problem). In academic dialogue, "winning" means coming to greater understanding.

Learning collaborative, productive dialogue in pursuit of truth and shared solutions requires us to make a paradigm shift: a change in the assumptions we make and the approaches we take. This paradigm shift is from seeing the state of college discourse as a national crisis of self-censorship, to a teaching problem that results from our extremely ambitious effort to educate the most diverse generation in recent US history at a time when polarization, disinformation, and mistrust characterize American life.

Changing our mindset from culture crisis to a matter of skills and competencies requires all of us to make three shifts in the way we imagine speech: first, de-emphasizing speech rights (even as we zealously protect them) and focusing on responsibilities. Second, responding to mistakes and harm with education and restorative measures, not with punitive reactions. And finally, seeing college as a place for collaborative inquiry, not combat and debate.

From Rights to Responsibilities

The First Amendment, by limiting government authority to regulate our speech, gives us the space to engage in deep and important conversations, even when it means sharing ideas that are challenging or disagreeable. This is, as the Supreme Court explained in *Texas v. Johnson*, a bedrock principle of our First Amendment, which protects our freedom to express ourselves even when we shock or offend our neighbors.

The First Amendment protects our freedom to learn from different or opposing views but it is up to each of us to decide how we *should* seek knowledge. Fictional works such as *Frankenstein* and *Jurassic Park* describe how science, thoughtlessly practiced, can lead to disaster. Although words are not like dinosaurs running rampant in human society, our choices about what we say have consequences. Contemporary experience shows us, for example, that misinformation can affect public health and safety.[3]

Even legally protected speech can have social, professional, or academic consequences. If you burn the flag in protest, your neighbor is free to disinvite you from her fourth of July party (a social consequence). If you're a political candidate, you might lose your election because you alienated voters who equate flag desecration with disrespect for our country (a professional consequence). And if you video yourself burning a flag and submit the video as a final project in a political

3. "New Analysis Shows Vaccines Could Have Prevented 318,000 Deaths," Brown School of Public Health and Microsoft AI for Health, May 13, 2022, https://globalepidemics.org/2022/05/13/new-analysis-shows-vaccines-could-have-prevented-318000-deaths/.

science class, you might receive a low grade—not because the professor disagrees with you, but because you were supposed to write a research paper (an academic consequence).

Sometimes we are willing to pay a cost for exercising our freedom of expression. Generations of activists have risked arrest and imprisonment for choosing to violate unjust laws (such as laws mandating segregated lunch counters). And politicians sometimes take unpopular stands knowing that they are likely to lose public support or professional allies and thus eventually, perhaps inevitably, their jobs. This book will not presume to tell readers there is one right way to exercise our freedom of expression or when to engage in civil disobedience. Instead, it will encourage you to understand the speech rights that our system of government protects and to consider the responsibilities that come with being the kind of student and civic participant you aspire to be.

From Punitive to Restorative Responses

Many American children are taught to respond to insults by saying "sticks and stones may break my bones, but words can never hurt me." This saying is meant to undermine the power of bullies by showing them that their taunts have no effect. I'll leave it to you to consider whether this strategy actually works and whether to encourage your own children or younger siblings to deploy it when faced with hurtful words.

It might be comforting, but the sentiment is not, strictly speaking, true. Words can do harm. The First Amendment protects some speech that inflicts emotional harm on individuals (including so-called hate speech) or expressions that harm society, such as by misinforming us about matters of public concern. Words can damage relationships, and relationships are necessary if we are going to address society's biggest problems, or just be happy people.

What we should do about the harm our speech might cause is a hard question worth considering. Many of us expect transgressions to result in punishment. In primary and secondary schools, rule-breakers face punishments such as detention, suspension, or even expulsion. including for speech that violates rules. As I will explain in Chapter 3, K-12 schools have a great deal of power to limit and punish student expression. Those of you who experienced primary and secondary education more recently than I did might have fresh memories of teachers or administrators wielding this authority. As you read this text and develop an impression about the relationship between expressive freedom and education, I encourage you to consider whether you agree with the system of limitations imposed earlier in your education. In the meantime, this text will help you understand and adopt the mindsets and practices that characterize scholarly inquiry and communication.

A community of inquiry, a place where adult learners recognize what they do not know, explore challenging questions, and try to solve seemingly intractable problems together, benefits from a different approach. In an academic community we presume all members are acting in good faith. When people are making good-faith efforts to learn and solve problems together, a community of inquiry responds to errors and transgressions with more inquiry, more speech, and more opportunities to learn and grow. Each member learns to show grace, and benefits from receiving grace as we strive and stumble through our journey to better understanding. We approach one another as colleagues, not competitors, and offer and receive the help we all need to develop our skills. Sincere apology, commitment to do better, shared responsibility, and deep listening—not punishment—together constitute a restorative approach.

From Debate to Inquiry

College discourse requires us to shift from a mindset of debate to inquiry. Debate involves opposing arguments being put forward and defended, often for an audience. In college classrooms, we are not opponents competing for voters' approval nor combatants in a judged performance. College classes are places for inquiry, which is a process of questioning. To be a student is to ask questions about the world around us; to question our own preformed opinions; and to interrogate our community's prevailing ideas and values. To debate is to prove that we are right. Inquiry requires us to understand what we do not yet know with certainty, and to entertain the idea that we might be wrong.

In short, being a scholar (and, I would argue, an engaged member of society) requires us to try to love the questions and learn to live in a state of curious uncertainty.

What Does It Take?

To develop a mindset of inquiry and build your skills as a reader, listener, and communicator, you will need to:

1. Learn to love the questions and to seek answers with integrity
2. Understand the rules and norms that apply to your conversations

3. Listen and read with a mindset of informed generosity and grace
4. Communicate to be understood
5. Engage in self-reflection

This book won't tell you what's okay to say and what isn't. Instead, as you explore these pages you will become more familiar with the rules and norms that govern academic and civic discourse—including the discourse of writing—and acquire tools to guide how to use your freedom and build your skills.

What's In It for Me?

The responsibilities that come with academic dialogue can seem very costly. Expressive freedom, by which I mean minimal regulation and restriction on what may be said, often requires us to be confronted by ideas we don't like and share space with people who don't like us. Restorative approaches to transgression can feel at odds with our social reality that conditions us to believe "justice" requires punishment. The exercises of inquiry and collaborative problem solving deny us the instant gratification that comes from certainty and winning an argument. As anyone who has spent time on social media can tell you, exercising intellectual humility and communicating with compassion are not a recipe for going viral. So why learn to love the questions themselves and try to master the skill of collaborative inquiry and responsible communication?

These are questions I particularly love, and which are at the core of my work on productive dialogue:

- Why does the First Amendment protect even unkind and cruel speech, and why should academic communities do the same (even in cases when they don't have to)?[4]
- Why take a restorative rather than punitive approach to speech that is "bad" or "wrong?"
- Why try to communicate responsibly and with compassion when sensationalism, name-calling, and inciting anger can lead to commercial and electoral success?

You and I might come to different conclusions about these questions. But I hope that you engage deeply with them as you read this book, and that you continue to consider them throughout college and life. I promise my students I won't grade them on the opinions they hold or the way they vote. And my hope is that this value comes through in your experience with this book. A thoughtful reading could lead you to conclude (as I have) that rules against profanity are silly. But maybe you will conclude that people who resort to profanity give insufficient weight to their responsibilities as communicators (if so, I hope you'll send me your thoughts; I am still a learner too, after all).

But I do know that this thing I'm encouraging you to try—to learn and practice productive civic dialogue—competes for attention with other priorities in our lives. You have other reading assignments, papers, jobs, and internships. The alluring sirens of censorship and performance, with their easy answers and quick rewards, are loud. So just this one time, as we get started, I'll explain why I think it's worth protecting expressive freedom; why I prefer grace to punishment; and why I believe we should

4. In Chapter 3 we will explore how public and private universities differ, and how context (classrooms, residence halls, online) affects the nature and extent of expressive freedom.

practice inquiry responsibly and kindly, rather than wield our expressive freedom like a club.

Why Protect Expressive Freedom and Practice Informed Generosity?

To quote Supreme Court Justice Anthony Kennedy, "times can blind us to certain truths and later generations can see that laws once thought necessary and proper in fact serve only to oppress."[5] Humans are imperfect. We can be hampered by the limits of our experience, and even our good-faith solutions to intractable problems can prove, upon further examination, to be wrong. In fact, often it's the things we all agree on that we get the most wrong.

Take, for example, our nation's policy response to drug addiction. In the 1970s through 1990s, the United States and many states enacted laws that led to mass incarceration. Support for these laws was bipartisan.[6] Arguably, to borrow Justice Kennedy's phrase, times blinded politicians across the political spectrum to the dangers of criminalizing addiction. Later generations have come to see that some of our laws in this realm are indeed oppressive. Today, drug law reform is becoming an uncommonly bipartisan area of interest,[7] even in our extremely polarized times.

5. *Lawrence v. Texas,* 539 U.S. 558, 123 S. Ct. 2472, 156 L. Ed. 2d 508 (2003).

6. The 1994 crime bill passed the US Senate by a vote of 95–4. "Roll Call Vote 103rd Congress—1st Session," United States Senate, https://www.senate.gov/legislative/LIS/roll_call_votes/vote1031/vote_103_1_00384.htm (accessed June 16, 2023).

7. "The State of Justice Reform 2018," Vera, https://www.vera.org/state-of-justice-reform/2018/bipartisan-support (accessed June 16, 2023).

If we are to understand the limitations of our wisdom, we need dialogue. Granting authorities the power to restrict criticism of dominant ideas can lead us to make even more mistakes—from unjust laws to unjust wars. If the passions of a moment can blind us to truth, we must rely upon each other to help us learn when and where we have been wrong. This requires freedom of expression.

In my own experience, hard conversations across principled differences have been some of the most rewarding in my life. There is no greater threat to excellent writing than unearned certainty; everything I have ever written—from my constantly evolving course syllabi to this book—has benefitted from critical dialogue. It is the tough conversations (as distinguished from the mean or dishonest ones) that produce the best ideas.

Why Grace Rather Than Punishment?

Let's be honest (dishonesty is inherently uncivil).[8] It feels good to see bad guys get punished. Anyone who has watched a movie can tell you that. Perhaps it's human nature to cheer for the bad guy to go to jail, or to be humiliated, or to face steep consequences by other means. Perhaps it's baked into our consciousness as members of a society that incarcerates an extraordinary percentage of its citizens.[9]

8. Dishonesty hinders productive inquiry and problem solving.

9. Wendy Sawyer and Peter Wagner, "Mass Incarceration: The Whole Pie 2022," Prison Policy Initiative, March 14, 2022, https://www.prisonpolicy.org/reports/pie2022.html.

Regardless of how satisfying or appealing it is to punish and shame transgression, I would posit that punishment is not the best answer to hurtful speech—even intentionally hurtful speech that falls short of harassment and threats. My primary reason for believing this is the same as my reason for teaching: I believe human beings are capable of learning what they didn't know and therefore capable of changing. And I believe college students in particular want to learn. The opportunity to learn means the opportunity to do better next time.

Beyond that, I have a very practical reason for opposing punishment for most hurtful speech: I believe society is better off if people continue to try to learn and work together in places like universities—even when they disagree—than if the people most in need of exposure to diverse human perspectives are exiled to places where they are unlikely to find them. I hope we can all spend more time exposed to the good-faith inquiry and dialogue that characterizes academic life.

A restorative approach is not without cost—particularly to those who are the most likely targets of hate or recipients of unwitting ignorance, people often from minoritized or marginalized groups. Reducing that cost is an important responsibility that students, faculty, and administrators should all make our mission.[10]

10. Like many advocates for expressive freedom, I am also conscious that speech restrictions adopted to make a school or society more inclusive can be used to suppress speech that people in power are opposed to.

Why Does Practicing Responsible Speech Make for a Better You, a Better University, and a Better World?

Learning is the engine of human progress. Freedom is essential to learning, but a learning community without academic standards ceases to be a learning community at all. Schools are, by definition, places that evaluate ideas. When I select a peer-reviewed journal article but not a conspiracy theory website for a course reading, I am expressing a core function of a university: to promote knowledge.

A learning community where some members know they are unwelcome cannot call itself a place for the free and robust exchange of ideas. When some members of the community are denigrated, when they must divert their energy to protecting themselves and educating peers, their opportunity to thrive diminishes—and with it, the community's access to their contributions diminishes too. Communicating in a way that respects all community members is essential to ensuring a truly open, productive dialogue.

Furthermore, the skill of communicating to be understood is an essential one beyond college. Whether we are representing a business to clients and customers, advocating for political change, providing medical advice and care, or navigating personal relationships, the capacity to communicate respectfully and effectively is essential.

Although to my knowledge most colleges do not have a civil discourse major or a required class on productive dialogue, inquiry and dialogue skills are fundamental to being an excellent college student and writer. Some of the most challenging aspects of college writing—including posing and answering original questions and deploying credible evidence accurately—are elements of constructive dialogue as well.

Finally, at a time when students (and teachers!) are burned out from standardized tests, , building resumes, and intense competition, I am suggesting an approach that encourages you to find ways to seek joy, excitement, and personal investment in what you are learning. When we love to learn, when we feel at ease with uncertainty, when we can see our classmates as fellow adventurers—not adversaries—we can love more than the questions. We can love our college experience. It is my hope that you find some ideas—and questions—to love on these pages.

Let's get started.

Discussion Questions and Classroom Exercises for Chapter 1

- What are your responsibilities as a class discussion participant? What are the professor's responsibilities? How do we support one another in meeting those responsibilities?
- What is the purpose of punishment in general? What is the purpose of punishment in a school setting?
- Under what circumstances is punishment the right response to student speech?
- Is there a topic related to this class that you would like to know more about?
- How hard is it for you to ask questions or say you don't know in a classroom space like this one?

- Practice saying "I don't know."
- An "I don't know" ice breaker: Student 1 asks a question that no other student could answer (e.g., what book am I reading for pleasure right now; what was my high school softball team's win-loss record) and calls on student 2. Student 2 answers "I don't know." It is now student 2's turn to ask a question and call on student 3. The exercise is complete when everyone has asked a question and responded "I don't know" in front of the class.

Writing Exercises for Chapter 1

- Imagine your ideal learning community. How would people treat one another? How would they handle disagreement? What would they accomplish in collaboration with one another? How would they address mistakes? How would they handle problems? What voices would you want to hear there? How would you bring those voices in?
- Who do you want to make proud? Picture the person you want to make proud—whether a parent, a mentor, a friend, or yourself. What would it take to make them proud? What will be challenging about that, for you? Are there times when being that best vision of yourself becomes harder?
- Write a mission statement for yourself. What do you want for yourself? What will you ask of yourself? How does your time in class fit into this mission?
- Consider a time when you have been wronged. Did you hope the wrongdoer was punished? What did you want to see happen? What was the resolution? If you had the

power to address the issue, what would you want? What would justice look like to you?

- Now consider a time when you violated a rule or wronged someone else. What were the consequences, if any? Do you think justice was served? If you were judging your own case, would you have ordered a punishment? Would you take some other approach?
- Select a topic about which you consider yourself reasonably well informed. What more could you learn or do you still need to know? What does it take to be an expert on this topic? Consider a question in your field of interest where many well-informed people disagree. Ask yourself: What would you—or someone new to the topic—need to know in order to form an opinion on the dispute?
- Set a goal for your reading, listening, and communicating this semester. What do you want to work on? What would success look like to you?

2

Try to Love the Questions and Seek Answers

An opinion is not an accomplishment.

—ME. I SAID THAT.

EVERY SEMESTER I ASK students to identify goals for the class, including their goals for writing and oral communication. One of the most common answers I receive is "I want to learn to support my opinions with evidence." To which I (gently) respond that this is a good start, but to take it to the next level, they need to build their opinions from evidence. I sincerely hope that if my students remember only one thing from my classes (or if you take only one message from this book), it's this:

> The work we do in college isn't showcasing and arguing for preformed opinions; it is identifying, exploring, and attempting to answer challenging questions with integrity.

If you are tired of endless arguments but interested in the subjects that people often argue about, this might be welcome news for you. If, on the other hand, you are extremely passionate about important subjects, and tired of being told to respect the other side's position even if it is disrespectful of who you are, then you should *also* welcome this news. Whether you have argument fatigue or false equivalence fatigue, pivoting from debate to inquiry (and position defense to position formation) will improve your experience with challenging subject matter.

Here's why: when we focus on inquiry, we are explorers and seekers—not constantly crouched in an argumentative or defensive posture. But unlike the brand of "both-sidesism" that characterizes media coverage of many important questions (which both serves to elevate falsehoods and to exclude many perspectives altogether), a posture of inquiry does not mean denying objective truth or conceding challenges to our humanity. In fact, lies and degradation can't survive rigorous inquiry.

To understand the difference between debate and the kind of inquiry we undertake in an academic setting, consider these two prompts about the same subject matter:

1. Should Springfield State University remove a Confederate monument from a central location on its Virginia campus?
2. Springfield State University was founded in 1805 in Virginia. You have been asked to serve on a committee that will make recommendations about how to educate students and the community about the school's complex history. What do you recommend?

The first question could be the subject of a debate. There appear to be two answers: yes and no. One might hope that people considering this question would engage thoughtfully about a wide variety of issues. However, it explicitly invites only a conclusion. No reason is offered for the monument to exist nor for you to be interested in it. Participants may bring whatever motivations they wish—from "owning the libs" to simply being contrary—to the conversation and are not asked to identify or explain them.

The first question also treats the monument as an isolated phenomenon, rather than as a part of a policy and history ecosystem that includes the campus and the world beyond. This question, as framed, does not invite people to engage with the challenging tasks of determining how complex historical figures such as Thomas Jefferson and George Washington (both presidents, Virginians, and enslavers) should be represented or under what circumstances they should or should not be honored. It is the kind of question that we might face in a voter referendum, but not a very scholarly one.

The second question looks like a more rewarding classroom exercise or writing assignment. There are infinite possible answers. Participants are not invited to join and play for one of two opposing teams; instead, they are invited to perform a useful service for everyone. Note also that in this exercise, participants are offered a reason for the work they are doing: teaching history. The prompt situates the immediate issue (whether to remove a Confederate monument) within a larger ecosystem: the school's history and Virginia and US history. It invites participants to consider a nearly limitless group of events, policies, people, and practices, and requires them to offer a principled method for educating others about them.

Although students' birthplaces, experiences, identities, and partisan preferences might predict how they respond to the first prompt,[1] these characteristics are unlikely to predict responses to the second. The second exercise asks students to inquire before taking a position, and to build an answer from infinite possibilities based upon what they learn. Students' backgrounds might still inform what they believe history consists of, but this will not necessarily predict their reactions to potential solutions, such as requiring Springfield State students to take a course in local history. Furthermore, the practice of inquiry that follows from this question enables students to work without a partisan agenda and to remain in a state of questioning while their work unfolds.

So What?

It turns out that some questions are inherently more lovable than others—they open avenues for exploration that are not possible in the binary, combative mindset that often characterizes partisan campaigns and debating. As a college student, you will not passively wait to be asked questions; you'll have more leeway (and responsibility) to identify and pursue challenging questions like this example than you did earlier in your educa-

1. According to a 2020 poll, there are partisan gaps in support for removing monuments; see Cameron Easley, "American Electorate Continues to Favor Leaving Confederate Relics in Place," Morning Consult, July 14, 2021, https://morningconsult.com/2021/07/14/confederate-statues-flag-military-bases-polling/.

tion. In fact, one of the most important skills you will master as a college student—particularly in liberal arts courses—is to ask and answer an original question in writing. You will find that if you craft questions that lend themselves to broad inquiry and nuanced answers, your work will be more rewarding and will better fulfill college-level expectations that you engage in analysis, synthesis, and original problem solving.

In this broader landscape of possibility, you can also find more ideas, texts, and questions that motivate you. This is one of the more lovable and exciting parts of college—your own curiosity plays a major role in what you end up writing and discussing.

Rejecting false binary questions won't just make you a better college student; it can help you become a more engaged community member and civic participant who resists and even reduces polarization. Polarization requires false binaries to thrive. In order to be fully polarized from one another, we have to be presented with only two choices. I am with you, or I'm against you. Some of our most polarized policy battles involve areas in which there is a great deal of room for nuanced policy and opinion but in which the issue has been given a provocative label and presented to the public as a binary choice between being two completely opposed sides.

Take, for example, "cancel culture." It is not often defined, but in general cancel culture means a cultural practice of inflicting inordinately harsh consequences on people as a result of their actions, words, or beliefs. How does false binary thinking work as an instrument of polarization when it comes to a concept like cancel culture? Consider the difference between a false binary question and a broader one.

False binary question: Is cancel culture out of control?

Broader question: Under what circumstances should people face social, academic, legal, or other consequences for their words, beliefs, or actions?

Almost all of us believe there are times when a person's behaviors, actions, or expressions of belief should have consequences. In fact, people who are concerned about cancel culture might believe that a tendency to unjustly cancel people should carry consequences (e.g., being roundly criticized). Similarly, almost all of us believe that some consequences for some actions and speech are unjust.

It is true that people will have strong disagreements over which actions, beliefs, or speech should carry consequences (and which consequences they should carry). But we are not members of warring pro- and anti-consequences factions. Terms like "cancel culture," however, and the false binary questions that animate discussions of nuanced problems (such as how to deal with our differences), place us in such separate camps. Resistance to false binary questions is resistance to polarization.

Pivoting from Yes/No to "Under What Circumstances"

To translate binary (debate) questions into more lovable questions, examine the issue represented by the question and write a question that includes a phrase like "under what circumstances." An example of a recent policy debate will show how this works.

In the height of the COVID-19 pandemic, mask mandates were a hotly disputed public policy. The question "Do you support mask mandates?" is a binary (yes/no) question that lends itself easily to debate. To find the implicit broader question, consider the purpose and substance of mask mandates. The purpose is to stop the spread of disease (and related injuries). The substance is a personal protective equipment (PPE) requirement. Add "under what circumstances," and the broader, inquiry-ready question is "Under what circumstances may authorities require people to wear PPE?"

You'll note that the term "mask mandate" does not appear in this question. You might also notice that this question will lead you to consider other policy questions that could help you explore the original one. For example, you might think about seat belt or helmet requirements and why they are permissible (or why you disagree with them). "Under what circumstances" also invites you to consider not only the power that authorities have to require PPE, but the responsibilities they might hold when requiring it. For example, you might conclude that hospital staff can be required to wear PPE only when the hospitals provide it and ensure that it meets certain standards of effectiveness.

From Isolated Decisions to Broader Principles (and Potential for Common Ground): Make Your Position a Rule

Sometimes you will be presented with a binary question and feel confident in your answer. For example, you might have a definitive position regarding your school's public health rules.

It is still possible to move from a binary position to a posture of inquiry. Doing so can not only help you better understand and explain your own position, it can help you determine the nature and extent of your disagreement with people who reach a different conclusion and defend your own approach if and when the time comes for a debate.

Here's how it works: make your position a rule.

While a position indicates your preferred outcome in a particular case, a rule is a decision-making tool that will apply to similar circumstances or disputes. For example, in baseball "Rodriguez is out" is a position an umpire may take in a game. The umpire's more broadly applicable rule is "when the ball is live and the runner is not touching the base, the runner may be tagged out."

"I support the mandate" is a position. When elected officials vote on measures like mask mandates, new taxes, or nondiscrimination laws, they might do so based on a broader rule or principle—for example, a city councilmember might oppose tax increases or criminalizing nonviolent conduct. But they can also make their decisions based on other considerations: constituent or donor preferences, previous promises, or their party's position. When we engage in inquiry, however, we explore a broader set of considerations and notice patterns and principles that might dictate our answer. When making an academic argument orally or in writing, utilizing a rule or principle—rather than a one-off position—helps us engage with critiques of our approach and refine our reasoning.

When you are writing a paper, the process of inquiry can also help you develop an original thesis statement and outline your arguments and counterarguments.

Turning your position into a rule requires you to explore and learn a range of related subject matter. It also requires you to consider all the competing interests that underlie the various positions and the priorities that explain how various parties value these interests.

From Positions to Interests

A position is what you say you want. An interest is why you want it.[2] The terms "position" and "interest" are frequently found in mediation, a process in which a neutral party facilitates discussion and agreement between disputing parties. When they come into a conversation, parties often express their positions. For example, a customer in a dispute with a restaurant where she got food poisoning might say: "This dump should not be in business!" Her interests could be ensuring no one else is injured, recouping lost time and expenses, and feeling vindicated. A trained mediator will help her articulate her interests and help her and the other party determine whether the initial position actually serves those interests.

Identifying the interests motivating your initial position will help you craft your rule. Continuing with our public health example, if you believe that the purpose of a mask mandate is to keep vulnerable people safe, you will develop a rule that requires masks when vulnerable people are present, but not require them when people are alone. Turning your position into a rule also helps you create a research plan. If you want to craft

2. Roger Fisher, William Ury, and Bruce Patton, *Getting to Yes*, 2nd ed. (New York: Penguin Putnam, 2006).

a rule that will achieve a specific interest (for example, reducing hospitalizations), you will need to conduct research on what type of measures are likely to achieve that result.

Making Your Position a Rule Helps Uncover Areas of Agreement and Shared Priorities

Although people on opposite sides of political binaries often harbor exceptionally strong feelings of support or opposition, the strength of their commitment does not tell us anything about the distance between their positions or the extent to which their underlying interests overlap or diverge. Turning your position into a rule enables you to locate the almost infinite range of possibilities outside the narrow (and sometimes politically partisan) binary and find the potential common ground you hold with people on the other side of that binary.

Put another way, binary questions mean all disagreements are 100 percent disagreements. But when we articulate a rule that answers an "under what circumstances" question, we learn much more about the participants' interests and values, including any common ground between them. To find a rule, we first need to articulate the broader, more lovable question behind our mask mandate binary question: "Under what circumstances can the school or city make people wear PPE?" Note that although there are firm yeses and nos for the binary question, very few people will create an absolutist rule on one side or another. The most extreme rules that we could create are:

- The city may force anyone to wear any kind of PPE regardless of the circumstances (e.g., they may require people to purchase and wear hazmat suits even when there is no pandemic).

And

- The city may never require anyone to wear any kind of PPE regardless of the circumstances (e.g., health professionals cannot be required to wear gloves while drawing blood; seat belt laws cannot be enforced).

Few people—regardless of the intensity of their support for or opposition to a mask policy—would support those extreme rules. Fortunately, there are nearly infinite alternatives between them. Although in politics, people might negotiate their way to a compromise, in college we consider alternatives through inquiry and dialogue. Because it is not necessary to reach a deal that binds classmates, there is little risk in acknowledging points of common ground or recognizing the validity of each other's points.

Collaboration Isn't the Same as Compromise: Recognize the Difference between Common Ground and Middle Ground

Sometimes the most passionate and principled students are concerned that the concept of civil discourse is about watering down their passion in the name of order or consensus. Constructive dialogue isn't about turning campus radicals into moderates, turning conservatives into liberals, or vice versa. As we'll explore later, there are some questions to which you might never open your mind (e.g., is the Earth flat; do I deserve fewer human rights than my classmates). But in a classroom, our default setting should be toward inquiry. To dispel the concern that dialogue requires moral compromise, it's useful to consider the difference between finding middle ground (as in a negotiation) and finding common ground, which students, teachers, and dialogue facilitators seek to do.

Middle ground is a point between two positions. When people work with mediators to resolve disputes, they often arrive at a middle ground between their opening proposals. In our food poisoning dispute, the customer might ask for $200 and a public apology, while the restaurant offers nothing. Eventually they reach a middle ground of $100—preferably based upon an objective standard for determining what the dispute is worth (such as the cost of medical care and lost time at work). Legislators sometimes negotiate compromises using these same principles. The final product might offer each side some, but not all, of what they asked for.

In college discussions, participants do not need to reach a middle ground. Instead, parties to a conversation seek common ground. Common ground is not a compromise between two positions; it means shared interests, values, motivations, and concerns. Take, for example, students who disagree about their school's "freshman forgiveness" policy, which allows students to drop a course where they performed poorly. They might not reach *middle ground* on a compromise rule, but they can find *common ground* as people who value fairness. Sometimes common ground means a common opponent; student groups who disagree about politics or culture might have shared complaints about the university administration. Or a shared problem—the same groups might be concerned about rising tuition.

In addition to shared values and concerns, common ground can include shared priorities, habits, and practices. The process of identifying common ground can help build trust and open the way to better communication. Something as simple as the class voting to include a ten-minute break halfway through their three-hour class meeting, or a project group devising a common note-taking system, helps students recognize that they have common ground. This is useful when we commit to adopt a mindset of generosity toward one another.

A love for music, art, being outdoors, or spending time with family are all examples of common ground we can hold with other students and community members. Although I hold no illusion that this common ground will be sufficient to create a bond of personal intimacy and trust necessary for close friendship, it can help build a foundation for respect and understanding. Respect—not friendship—is a necessary condition for constructive collaborative inquiry.

On college campuses, we have built-in common ground as scholars. But campuses aren't a refuge from the kinds of conflict (and even hate) that exist off campus. The question "Under what circumstances is there enough common ground for dialogue?" is yours to explore, utilizing the same process of inquiry you apply to other hard questions. Although I find that seeking common ground is immensely useful, there are limits to what I would ask of students in this regard. I don't expect you to seek common ground with a serial killer over your shared love of mint chocolate chip ice cream, nor to engage with people who dehumanize or belittle you. When I explore the benefits and limits of listening generously, I will explore what other limitations each of us might find in our capacity for dialogue.

College-Level Standards and a Mindset of Inquiry

As you progress in your education, you are asked to demonstrate increasingly sophisticated types of learning. In the early years you learn to line up for recess, ask to use the restroom, and share crayons. In elementary school you engage in rote learning, such as memorizing multiplication tables or state capitals. Assessments (such as quizzes and worksheets) require you only to demonstrate that you remember what you have learned. As the years go by, the tasks evolve from simple recall to higher-order thinking. In college, academic expectations should reflect a higher order of complexity than before. Your mindset of inquiry will help you meet them.[3] Bloom's taxonomy[4] is a useful way to describe the levels of learning and show you the kind of work that happens in a college course.

The most basic level of learning is simple recall (e.g., Lincoln was the sixteenth US president). After recall comes understanding (Lincoln's Emancipation Proclamation was an executive order); then application (in a future war, a president could issue emergency executive orders). The most complex and advanced

3. Andrea Brenner and Lara Schwartz, *How to College*, 1st ed. (St. Martin's, 2019).

4. Patricia Armstrong, "Bloom's Taxonomy," Vanderbilt University, 2010, https://cft.vanderbilt.edu/guides-sub-pages/blooms-taxonomy/.

learning skills include analysis, synthesis, and creating original work.

In college courses, we most often do that higher-order work—analyzing, comparing, critiquing, and creating. We might use the beginning of class time to check that people know the facts and understand the concepts being taught before proceeding to discussions where we apply concepts and rules, compare texts with varying or contradictory approaches, and evaluate the ideas presented in course readings. Often, and particularly in upper-level seminars, students need to demonstrate the highest level in the taxonomy—making, explaining, and defending an original claim in a paper or presentation.

The practice of inquiry—in which students consider questions in all their complexity, identify related issues, explore patterns, and develop and apply principles—is the engine for this kind of college-level work. How do we do it? We start with the most common correct answer in the world, and then ask one of the most productive questions.

Intellectual Humility

Pop quiz:

What is the most common correct answer in the history of the known universe?

a. I'm not too sure.
b. Is it yes?
c. Umm, no?
d. **I don't know.**

Not knowing—and being excited about the possibility of finding out—is the default state for scholars, from first-year college students to postdoctoral researchers. I have found that the more accomplished a person is, the less likely they are to claim to be an expert on anything beyond their specialty.[5] Achieving expertise in anything—from First Amendment law to shoeing horses—often means developing respect for how complex any one topic can be.

On the other hand, people who know a little bit about something often claim to be experts. Sometimes, as with opinion columnists or commentators, presenting a position is their job. Sometimes, as with friends or relatives who "did their own research," confident and forceful opinions reflect false certainty and lack of familiarity with how complex a question really is.

For the rest of us, there are other reasons why it's hard to say "I don't know." It's understandable that students find it hard to show intellectual humility in front of one another after a lifetime of being ranked against one another based on tests and grades. The competition for college admissions and scholarships requires students to make an impression of competence and achievement. Intellectual humility can seem counterproductive to the goal of getting ahead. And thanks to social media, most people with internet access can become a published author and purveyor of opinions.

5. Mariana V. C. Coutinho, Justin Thomas, Alia S. M. Alsuwaidi, and Justin J. Couchman, "Dunning-Kruger Effect: Intuitive Errors Predict Overconfidence on the Cognitive Reflection Test," Frontiers in Psychology, April 8, 2021, https://www.frontiersin.org/articles/10.3389/fpsyg.2021.603225/full.

My students have pointed out that it can feel like there is a risk in *not* having an opinion: people could think you are ignorant or simply don't care. And yet it is uncertainty and openness to input—not certainty—that is the mark of someone who is serious about a topic. For all these reasons, the state of uncertainty, which is central to the college experience, can make students feel vulnerable.[6] This is one reason I ask my students to practice saying "I don't know" in front of each other early in the semester, and encourage you to practice too.

As one of my students explained, in this culture, "you have to know everything, to be 100 percent certain. I'm trying to give myself the grace to change my opinion."[7]

The state of understanding what we don't know—intellectual humility—opens infinite possibilities for exploration and, therefore, joy.

The Threshold Question: What Would We Need to Know?

Forming positions and developing preferences based on evidence—as opposed to hunting for evidence to support preexisting positions—is a core competency of college-level work. Many excellent books have been written about how to

6. This pressure, not uncommon for students just out of high school who participated in selective admissions processes, does not affect everyone. Students and faculty alike can benefit from reflecting on whether this mindset affects people in their classroom.

7. Alicia Talamas interview with Lara Schwartz, American University, March 3, 2023.

conduct research—a process that is distinct from entering a question or topic into a search engine and deploying our favorite results in conversation.[8] The various academic disciplines have their own discipline-specific research methods. For example, legal research includes finding applicable *authority*—statutes, regulations, and judicial precedent. Social science research involves interviews, surveys, and other means of acquiring quantitative and qualitative data about the phenomenon being studied. Laboratory research involves still other distinct methods of gathering information.

Your major might require a research methods course. Even if it's not required, consider taking a research methods class. Not only will it enable you to practice research, it can also help you learn to read, analyze, and evaluate published research. This book does not replace your research methods class, but rather introduces you to some habits of mind that will help make research more meaningful and rewarding.

The first habit that enables us to pivot from position defense (debate) to position formation (inquiry) is asking "What would I need to know?" When presented with a claim, ask "What would we need to know in order to determine whether that claim is accurate?" You can also use this question to organize research tasks in connection with a project, asking "What would we need to know to be ready to write about or propose solutions in this area of inquiry?"

Let's look at the classroom exercise from the beginning of this chapter: the Confederate monument at (fictitious) Springfield

8. For example, Wayne Booth, Gregory C. Columb, and Joseph M. Williams, *The Craft of Research*, 4th ed. (Chicago: University of Chicago Press, 2016).

State University. Our threshold question, what would we need to know in order to determine what to do about the monument, could lead us to inquire about the monument's origin; historical literacy among students and community members; the existence of other historical markers; the school's curriculum; the cost of moving or demolishing a monument; other institutions' responses to questions like this; and federal, state, or local laws protecting historical monuments and artworks.

Asking what we need to know is also a tool for facilitating dialogue. When you are inspired to call BS, a less confrontational alternative is to ask, "What would we need to know in order to consider this claim?" You get the same result—pivoting to interesting, productive questions—without putting the speaker on the defensive.

Each of these subjects could lead you to additional questions—and all might involve discipline-specific research methods.

Questions Beget Questions (and Disagreement)

When you engage in collaborative inquiry with classmates, you will run into questions for which there are no clear-cut answers. For example, in our monument exercise, one group could explore the monetary cost of removing a monument. But the question of whether removing the monument is worth the money will be much harder to answer.

Another working group might research the impact the monument has on community members, conducting surveys on whether the monument affects the university's reputation or deters or attracts prospective students. They might arrive at an answer that helps contextualize the dollar figure that the first group came to. Even so, the full group will still have to engage in dialogue about the competing priorities and values that inform what decision is made.

A Favorite Question—Where Would You Draw the Line?

Line-drawing questions help us find the limitations of our claims. For example, if I state, "I support expressive freedom on campus," a line drawing question asks me if there are any circumstances when that would not be true. In response, I would clarify that I support expressive freedom, subject to legal limitations such as those found in harassment and nondiscrimination laws.

Before making a claim, ask yourself a line-drawing question, and explore the contours and limits of what you are asserting. Engaging with the limitations of your claim demonstrates higher-order reasoning. When you explain your limiting reasoning, you also demonstrate to listeners that you have engaged in good-faith analysis.

Questions That Reflect Objective Standards

Although in political conversations we can take a position or cast a vote for any reason (or for no reason at all), in an academic setting, we ground our analysis in some objective standard. For example, in casual conversation we might say Springfield State is a "good" college. Scholars of higher education would attempt to define "good," measuring factors such as student satisfaction, research output, or graduation rates (and other scholars might critique this definition of "good" and propose alternatives). The questions "How does this college serve its community?" and "What does this college contribute to a body of knowledge?" are more fruitful for academic inquiry than "Is this college good?"

Questions That Critically Examine Conclusions That Are Presented as Objective

Continuing the example about what makes a "good" college, we can engage in another form of inquiry—exploring what values, priorities, or assumptions are reflected in a text.

College rankings illustrate this. They often rank colleges by selectivity—the more applicants a college rejects, the higher its ranking. Defining "good" to mean selective is a value judgment, not a scientific reality. Whether it is a useful proxy for "good" and whether it has unintended or intended negative consequences on education are both excellent questions. They bring us back to our foundational research question: What would we need to know to determine whether selectivity is associated with better education? Exploring this question is an example of the kind of critical thinking found in excellent papers.

Questions That Draw upon Different Disciplinary Lenses

Academic disciplines are not about differing subject matter—they are about different modes of inquiry. We might tell a grade school student who loves the ocean that they should study marine biology. At the college level, we could point them to multiple *disciplines*.

- Economists study the costs and benefits of fishing.
- Psychologists study why fear of sharks has an outsized impact on people's risk assessment.
- Sociologists study why more women die in tsunamis than men.
- Anthropologists study how the dangers of erosion are understood by particular communities.
- Historians study how oceanic trade routes have affected human events.
- Literature scholars study works such as *Moby Dick* and *Beloved*.
- Marine biologists study the life forms that live in the ocean.

Each academic discipline involves a distinct approach. Coursework in multiple disciplines helps build your inquiry skills. Even when you are studying and writing for a specific academic course, considering your subject through multiple disciplinary lenses enables you to appreciate how complex the subject matter is and to approach it using distinct tools for understanding it.

Take the subject that inspired this book: expression on college campuses. Much of the conversation to date has been legalistic. This is not completely unreasonable; laws define the extent of our freedom of expression. With all due respect to lawyers (I am one), the law cannot tell us all we need to know about inquiry and dialogue.

Where Would *I* Draw the Line? Less Lovable Questions

The idea of loving the questions themselves has inspired me since I was in college, when a friend gave me *Letters to a Young Poet* (the source of this book's title). Loving an idea comes with its own perils. The danger that "times can blind us to certain truths" is greater when we have a deep attachment to an idea. Thus, when I started working on this book, I followed my own advice and asked questions designed to find the limitations of the idea of loving questions and welcoming uncertainty. I sought out people whom I knew would be skeptical. My process of inquiry led me to identify two major categories of limitations: bad-faith questioning and misleading questions (whether asked in bad faith or out of imprecision).

Bad Faith

When challenged on his baseless claims, one prominent conspiracy theorist used to claim he was just asking questions no one else would ask. This framing presents lying as bravely challenging orthodoxy. Willingness to challenge dominant ideas is essential to academic thinking, but this "just asking questions" approach, when used to obfuscate baseless claims, is the opposite of inquiry.

Though it's easy to say bad-faith questions don't count, the truth is that even arguments presented in bad faith can be worth exploring. In addition, defining "bad faith" is hard. We could consider the questioner's intent. Do they intend to advance knowledge or derail the conversation? Refine an idea or confuse and mislead? Sometimes the answer is obvious. Still, as a lawyer, I know that intent can be hard to discern, much less prove. Evaluating the question itself can be easier. Here are a few types of bad-faith question:

- No basis in fact ("just asking" if a vaccine includes a tracking device, or whether there is a child sex abuse ring run out of the basement of a pizza restaurant that actually has no basement)
- Creating a trap ("When did you stop cheating on exams?")
- False binary choice ("Do you salute the flag or disrespect veterans?")

In a dialogue, we can try to reframe or improve these questions rather than try to litigate intent. A question with no basis in fact might present an opportunity to correct the record (including by asking "What would we need to know in order to verify that claim?") or explore the questioner's underlying concern. We can reshape a false binary question into a more lovable one.

Lovable Questions and Information Literacy

"Information literacy" refers to the skills and habits required to identify, evaluate, interpret, and use information. As a first step toward information literacy, it is important to understand that some sources are more credible than others. For example, when writing a college paper, students should cite peer-reviewed journal articles, not YouTube conspiracy videos. Distinguishing credible sources from noncredible sources is an essential college-level practice—particularly in an era where misinformation and disinformation proliferate.[9]

Your college library is a great resource for learning to identify credible sources. In my experience, students who use library resources—from online research tutorials to librarian information sessions and office hours—find this effort rewarding and useful.

Information literacy isn't only about distinguishing between credible and noncredible sources. It also involves understanding how to interpret and deploy data and evaluate whether the evidence presented supports the claim for which it is being used. Anyone who has ever used a search engine knows there is a difference between finding *an* answer and finding *the* answer (if such a thing exists). Inquiry consists of more than just using a search engine. In addition to discipline-specific research methods, try the following practices.

Seek a Broad Understanding about Your Field of Inquiry First

Having a basic understanding of how various disciplines approach questions enables us to better evaluate the information we find. For example, in law, it's important to know that the Supreme Court does not have to defer to lower court decisions.

9. David Ardia, Evan Ringel, Victoria Smith Ekstrand, and Ashley Fox, "Addressing the Decline of Local News, Rise of Platforms, and Spread of Mis- and Disinformation Online," UNC Center for Media Law and Policy, University of North Carolina at Chapel Hill, December 2020, https://citap.unc.edu/local-news-platforms-mis-disinformation/.

When evaluating social science research, it's useful to understand how sample sizes affect studies and to be familiar with the major events that could render older research out of date (for example, we would want to know whether a study of Americans' perceptions about terrorism risk was from before or after September 11, 2001).

Evaluate Information for Bias

In my experience, students often inaccurately define the term "bias" to mean anything other than complete neutrality. I conduct a class exercise where students evaluate potential witnesses for a legislative hearing about the minimum wage. One potential witness is a labor economist whose work tends to support minimum wage increases. Invariably, some students state that the economist is biased because they have a position about the minimum wage. However, there is a difference between *bias* and *expertise*. Bias does not mean a preference for one solution over another. Firefighters are not *biased* against throwing gasoline on fires—they are experts in putting fires out. Rather than defining bias to mean the absence of a position, I define bias as any factor that might make the information (or its source) less trustworthy.

An author's financial or personal stake in the outcome is one type of bias. For example, if research on solar panels is funded by a solar panel company (or, conversely, by the fossil fuel industry), we have reason to doubt the findings. Bias also has discipline and field-specific definitions. Professional codes of ethics and conduct define bias for doctors, judges, attorneys, journalists, auditors, and others.

Understand the Utility and Limitations of Information

Even if a source is credible, information literacy also means understanding the utility and limits of the information we find. When presented with a data point, it is important to ask, "What is it possible to conclude from this piece of information?" To see what I mean, consider this data point about expressive freedom: "Only 34 percent of Americans said they believed that all Americans enjoyed freedom of speech completely."[10]

The *New York Times* cited this in support of a claim that America has a "free speech problem."[11] However, people who understand free speech know that it is not unlimited. The survey could plausibly show that many respondents understand expressive freedom has limits or that some do *not* understand this. The response could be seen as an acknowledgment that some Americans (such as incarcerated people, students in K-12 schools, or active-duty military in uniform) have legally diminished rights to express themselves. Furthermore, the question only measures respondents' perceptions—not how much expressive freedom people actually have.

Get in the habit: when considering an argument that uses data to support a claim, check whether the data and claim are

10. "Free Speech Poll," The *New York Times*/Siena College Research Institute, February 22, 2022, https://int.nyt.com/data/documenttools/free-speech-poll-nyt-and-siena-college/ef971d5e78e1d2f9/full.pdf.

11. Editorial Board, "America Has a Free Speech Problem," *New York Times*, March 18, 2022, https://www.nytimes.com/2022/03/18/opinion/cancel-culture-free-speech-poll.html.

fully matched. Ask: What does this data prove? What more would I need to know to conclude that the claim is true?

Understand How Imprecisely (or Misleadingly) Framed Questions Can Limit the Value of Answers

Loving the questions can also mean recognizing that there are some questions that could lead to inherently less truthful answers. Here are some examples:

Questions That Plant the Seeds of a Desired Outcome

A poll asked, "How much of a problem is it that some Americans do not exercise their freedom of speech in everyday situations out of fear of retaliation or harsh criticism?"[12] This question describes something that sounds like a problem, then asks respondents to evaluate its seriousness. Using poll questions in this fashion is called priming.[13]

This question illustrates another characteristic of unreliable questions: undefined terms. What does "retaliation" mean? Does it include acceptable or even desirable consequences (such as firing someone for sexual harassment)? Or does it include only the legal definition of retaliation? Does "fear" mean fear for one's safety or fear of social consequences? Does "harsh" criticism mean unjustifiably harsh, or severe but true

12. See Editorial Board, "America Has a Free Speech Problem."

13. Michael Parkin, "Priming," in *Encyclopedia of Survey Research Methods*, ed. Paul J. Lavrakas (Thousand Oaks, CA: Sage Publications, 2008), 611–612.

criticism? Does "exercise freedom of speech" mean asserting one's conscience in defiance of popular opinion or uttering horrific but constitutionally protected insults? Undefined terms limit the utility of the answers because we have no way of knowing how respondents interpreted the vague question.

False Binaries and Oversimplification

Some questions frame complex topics as simple ones, particularly by presenting a false binary choice. My favorite example is a poll question that asks respondents whether they prefer the Supreme Court to base its rulings on what the constitution "meant as originally written" or on what it "means in current times."[14] This question has been used to distinguish between what are popularly understood to be the conservative (constitution as written) and liberal (change with the times) views of our Constitution. Many lawyers, including me, would offer another option: that the Constitution was originally written to be flexible to the time we're in. Language such as "unreasonable searches and seizures" and "cruel and unusual punishment" can reasonably be understood to have some relationship to accepted practices.

In fact, justices across the political spectrum have interpreted some provisions of our Constitution with reference to the times. Even the late Justice Antonin Scalia, considered a role model for Conservative judicial thought, attributed constitutional

14. Kristen Bialik, "Growing Share of Americans Say Supreme Court Should Base Its Rulings on What Constitution Means Today," Pew Research Center, May 11, 2018, https://www.pewresearch.org/fact-tank/2018/05/11/growing-share-of-americans-say-supreme-court-should-base-its-rulings-on-what-constitution-means-today/.

significance to handguns' popularity for self-defense in the home among twenty-first-century Americans.[15]

Regardless of where we lie on the ideological spectrum or what we think about judicial decisions on guns, criminal justice, or other hot-button issues, the question serves us all poorly. Either by impact or by design, it describes a false binary that oversimplifies a complex matter. Although political combatants might not find middle ground on the policy issues related to these questions, scholars should seek common ground in having a more nuanced conversation. A scholar would ask "Under what circumstances do judges look to prevailing conditions in interpreting the Constitution?" and find rich avenues for exploration.

Blurring the General and the Specific

Questions that trick respondents into thinking they're debating a general point when the debate is about the nature and extent of exceptions can also yield misleading results. For example, when asked "Should we protect Second Amendment rights?" most respondents say yes. In isolation, their answer could be "proof" that gun safety regulation is not popular. But when we ask more specific questions, such as "Should we require background checks for gun purchases?" large majorities say yes. The general terms "gun control" and "Second Amendment" are too vague to be useful in gauging public opinion. This is another reason academic dialogue can be more rewarding than political discourse. A well-crafted paper or classroom discussion will engage more deeply with

15. *District of Columbia v. Heller*, 554 U.S. 570 (2008).

specifics, not only with vaguely worded concepts that have emotional appeal.

Implying an Imaginary Golden Age

Questions that imply a new problem without providing a point of comparison can also distort results. For example, "Are young people today too sensitive to offense?" implies that previous generations behaved differently. Note that this is arguably a subset of the first category, questions that prime a desired outcome by hinting at a problem.

When posing research questions, learn to structure them like a researcher in your academic discipline. Attune yourself to the questions asked in the research you read and make a practice of testing whether approaching a question from a different angle (or discipline) could lead to a more nuanced analysis.

Note for writers: Be vigilant against the temptation to oversimplify your questions. One way to protect yourself against crafting a misleading research question (or paper thesis) is to run it by your professor in office hours. It can also help to workshop ideas with a classmate.

Discussion Questions and Classroom Exercises for Chapter 2

- Select a topic from the course syllabus, from the day's readings, from current events, or from your course community guidelines and policies. Identify a question or point of difference that is currently phrased as a binary (e.g., Will hateful slurs be tolerated in this classroom?). Create an "under what circumstances" question (e.g., Under what circumstances could hateful slurs be present in the classroom?).

- Explore your "under what circumstances" question and define the contours and limitations of an answer that applies broadly (e.g., if slurs appear in a work of literature, government document, archival source, or artwork being studied, they may be present in the classroom).
- Identify a topic that you consider difficult to discuss in class. What common ground, if any, do students share when it comes to this topic? What interests and values motivate your ideas on the topic? What interests and values motivate others? Discuss the interests and values that motivate you and your peers.
- Where do you draw the line between healthy confidence and false certainty?

Writing Exercises

- *Rankings and information literacy*: Find an article that ranks something of interest to you. What criteria are used to create the ranking? What values are reflected in the ranking system? What is missing? If you were creating a ranking, what would your criteria be?
- *Multidisciplinary thinking*: The University of Springfield is a private university in Virginia. In fall 2021 a U of S student wore a Confederate flag t-shirt to the dining hall. Several students told him the t-shirt was hurtful, saying the Confederate flag symbolizes slavery. Consider how various academic disciplines would approach this episode.

3

Understand the Rules and Norms of College Discourse

UNDER WHAT CIRCUMSTANCES is speech protected or unprotected on college campuses and elsewhere?

> Congress shall make no law respecting an establishment of religion, or prohibiting the free exercise thereof; or abridging the freedom of speech, or of the press; or the right of the people peaceably to assemble, and to petition the Government for a redress of grievances.
>
> —US CONSTITUTION, AMENDMENT I

> College and university teachers are citizens, members of a learned profession, and officers of an educational institution. When they speak or write as citizens, they should be free from institutional censorship or discipline, but their special position in the community imposes special obligations.
>
> —AMERICAN ASSOCIATION OF UNIVERSITY PROFESSORS 1940 STATEMENT OF PRINCIPLES ON ACADEMIC FREEDOM AND TENURE[1]

1. "1940 Statement of Principles on Academic Freedom and Tenure," American Association of University Professors, https://www.aaup.org/report

To a degree, academic freedom is a reality today because Socrates practiced civil disobedience.

—MARTIN LUTHER KING JR., "LETTER FROM BIRMINGHAM JAIL"[2]

Free Speech on Campus Changed Its Relationship Status to "It's Complicated"

As you've prepared for college, you've likely heard conflicting ideas about whether college is a place where "free speech" (whatever that is) is welcomed or suppressed. Student protests of controversial speakers have made national headlines,[3] and surveys show mixed feelings about whether campuses are places where the free exchange of ideas can thrive.[4]

Short answer: it's complicated. "Free speech" in college includes expression rights protected by the First Amendment to the US Constitution and defined and limited by judicial decisions; institutional policies on expression and dissent; a concept called "academic freedom" that particularly applies to

/1940-statement-principles-academic-freedom-and-tenure (accessed June 16, 2023).

2. Martin Luther King Jr., *Letter from Birmingham Jail* (San Francisco: Harper San Francisco, 1994).

3. Evan Gertsmann, "Protests, Free Expression, and College Campuses," *Social Education* 82, no. 1 (2018): 6–9.

4. "Free Expression on Campus: A Survey of U.S. College Students and U.S. Adults," Knight Foundation, April 2016, https://knightfoundation.org/wp-content/uploads/2016/04/FreeSpeech_campus-1.pdf.

scholarship; ethical rules binding researchers; discipline-specific writing rules (such as how to cite evidence); academic integrity (rules against plagiarism and cheating); state and federal laws on harassment and discrimination; and classroom conduct norms (for example, no *ad hominem* attacks).

This chapter will explore and explain the rules and norms that govern expression. It is a description of the rules as they are—not a judgment about what they should be. As you read, apply your habits of inquiry; make note of what more you need to know and what you think of these rules.

"Campus Speech" Actually Takes Placed in a Wide Variety of Contexts, Many with Their Own Rules

The extent of our freedom of expression depends upon context. For example, there are strict rules against even joking about weapons in an airport security line, speech that would be protected from censorship in a movie or play. Governments are generally allowed to make content-neutral rules about the time, place, or manner of speech. Here are some examples of time, place, and manner restrictions:

- A ban on using megaphones or other amplification devices near a hospital at night.
- No talking in the library.
- Signs and flyers may be posted only on bulletin boards, not taped or nailed to walls.

To understand the rules of "campus speech," we must consider that college life contains multiple different speech contexts. There are spaces that function like a town square, such as the campus quadrangle; spaces that are like homes, such as residence halls; commercial and workspaces such as a campus shop; government programs such as the Reserve Officer Training Corps (ROTC); private associations such as fraternal organizations; and academic contexts, such as classes. One student might be a nursing major; a member of a fraternal organization; a student senator; a roommate; and an ROTC cadet. All these roles and contexts come with varying expressive rights and responsibilities: from academic integrity rules in nursing classes to uniform regulations for ROTC training.

Inquiry and Standards: Values in Balance

Our commitment to the exchange of ideas is a common feature of higher education.[5] Higher education offers more freedom of expression than many other places. As I will explain, students in K-12 schools are subject to significant restrictions on expression. Anyone who has held a job knows that workplaces often restrict expression: a worker might not remain employed for long if they told customers the competitors' products were better or tweeted about clients' personal problems.[6]

5. "Mission," American Association of University Professors, https://www.aaup.org/about/mission-1 (accessed June 16, 2023).

6. Employers' power to limit expression is not unlimited. For example, federal, state, and local laws protect workers' right to speak up about discrimination or dangerous work conditions.

Standards are also a benchmark of higher education, which means our freedom to express ideas is in some ways inherently less free in college than on public sidewalks or in our homes—where no one can mark us down for making a false claim, failing to cite evidence, or borrowing someone else's idea without attribution. Selective admissions, grading, selective scholarship programs, and peer review of research are all mechanisms by which higher education evaluates ideas and expression.

These two values of higher education—open inquiry and rigorous standards—have been present and central to the college experience since long before speech on campus became a highly visible, highly polarized issue. It is important to understand these twin pillars of campus expression so that we know where our speech rights begin and end.

What Do We Mean by Free Speech?

"Free speech" is popularly understood to mean that people can't be persecuted for what they say. It is not a precise legal term, however. There are (at least) two reasons the term "free speech" is inadequate for our exploration of campus discourse. First, it is too narrow. "Speech" is commonly understood to mean talking. But on campus and elsewhere, the activities covered by "speech" rights are much broader.

Consider these situations:

- An athlete takes a knee during the national anthem.
- A social media company bans classified ads for animals or guns on its platform.
- A high school student wears a t-shirt with a beer brand logo.

- A consumer boycotts a national restaurant chain.
- A group of people marches through a public official's neighborhood, carrying signs and chanting.
- A singer-songwriter tells a political candidate he may not play her songs at rallies.
- A national fraternal organization announces that it has cut ties with a local chapter.
- A student organization invites a controversial political figure to deliver a speech at a university.
- Another student organization protests outside the lecture hall where the above speech is taking place.
- A college dean wears a hijab or a yarmulke at work.
- A professor criticizes an activist group on Twitter.

These are all examples of expression or expressive conduct. The people and groups are conveying thoughts, feelings, or ideas—whether with words, images, actions, the company they keep, or a combination of those things. The entire academic enterprise is a series of expressive acts—class lectures and discussions, papers and presentations, study sessions, conversations with friends, campus activism, and student groups all involve expression. Even your choice to wear a college logo shirt is a form of expression.

The concept we most often call "free speech" is more accurately called freedom of expression. The First Amendment to the United States Constitution protects expression—including speaking, writing, artistic expression, reading, expressive conduct, and our choice of the company we keep (called association) from government interference and punishment. To be considered expressive conduct that might be protected by the First Amendment, an action must be (a) intended to convey a particular message; and (b) likely to be understood by those who viewed it.[7] When nongovernment actors (such as private social media companies or employers) limit our speech, the First Amendment is not implicated (but the impact could be just as important to us).

Check your comprehension:

As she is walking onto the court before a game, a basketball player notices her shoe is untied. She gets down on one knee to tie her shoe as the national anthem begins. She finishes tying her shoe and stands up.

Is kneeling to tie her shoe "expressive conduct?" Explain.[8]

Expressive freedom also includes the freedom *not* to speak. In striking down a law that required public school students and teachers to salute the flag, the Supreme Court famously wrote, "if there is any fixed star in our constitutional constellation, it is that no official, high or petty, can prescribe what shall be orthodox in politics, nationalism, religion, or other matters of opinion or force citizens to confess by word or act their faith therein."[9] Freedom not to speak (known as free-

7. See *United States v. O'Brien*, 391 U.S. 367 (1968).

8. Applying the rule from *US v. O'Brien*, the player did not intend to convey a message by kneeling. However, some members of the audience might have thought she intended to convey a message, because some players take a knee during the anthem to express an opinion.

9. *West Virginia Bd. of Ed. v. Barnette*, 319 U.S. 624 (1943).

dom from compelled speech) is part of expressive freedom, including on college campuses.

Schools are free to adopt and teach institutional values. For example, they can declare (accurately) that tobacco is unhealthy, adopt rules against tobacco use, and include anti-tobacco messages in their student and employee orientations. But if a school requires community members to say they believe that tobacco is bad, that crosses the line into compelled speech.

Academic Freedom

Universities are communities of inquiry dedicated to learning, teaching, and research. Community members develop, publish, dispute, and defend theories; study and challenge cultural ideas and government structures and laws; produce and interpret art, music, and literature; and teach and learn complex subject matter and skills. Academic freedom enables this inquiry by protecting university faculty's right to research, publish, teach, and exercise their speech rights as citizens free from official interference. For example, it protects a faculty member's choice to conduct research on a topic such as human sexuality or racial discrimination. It also protects their right to speak out on matters of public concern without risking their jobs.

Faculty have the right to academic freedom and the responsibility to meet professional standards. A biology professor is expected to understand biology. Faculty hired to teach writing are expected to dedicate class time to writing instruction. Academic freedom does not protect expression that tends to demonstrate faculty are not competent in their teaching field.

Check your comprehension:

Which of these is protected by academic freedom?

- A medical school professor tweets that most vaccines are more dangerous than the diseases they are supposed to prevent.
- A psychology professor conducts research about sex offenders and publishes a paper recommending therapy rather than imprisonment.
- An admissions office staff member publishes a blog calling for legacy admissions preferences to be abolished.
- An accounting professor spends several class periods discussing current events with students, rather than teaching accounting.[10]

Not So Much "Free" as Protected

The term "free speech" is also too broad and imprecise. The term gives the impression that any limitation on speech is antithetical to the First Amendment. This is not the case; many forms of expression are not legally protected. As University of California at Riverside professor Carlos Cortes explains, "through more than two centuries of laws, regulations, and

10. Only the second item is covered by academic freedom. The first professor is not meeting professional standards in their field. The admissions staff member is not a college instructor (they might be covered by their school's free expression policy, however). The accounting professor is not teaching.

court decisions, we have created a system of robust but legally restrained speech."[11]

Furthermore, even protected expression can have consequences. Let's say I place a yard sign in front of my house to show my support for a ballot initiative to decriminalize cannabis possession. This is a form of protected expression; the government cannot punish me for my position nor ban yard signs that support decriminalization while permitting the opposition to post their signs. However, nongovernment actors, from employers to social organizations, might conclude my position is incompatible with their mission or values, and exclude me.[12]

Finally, "free speech" comes with costs. It can spread disinformation that puts people in harm's way, cause emotional distress, and be more burdensome to certain community members than others. I have concluded that freedom of expression is preferable to the alternative. But it is not close to free.[13]

I will therefore refer to protected or unprotected speech and expression rather than "free speech."

11. Carlos E. Cortés, "Beyond Free Speech: Fostering Civic Engagement at the Intersection of Diversity and Expression," University of California Free Speech Center, March 2019, https://freespeechcenter.universityofcalifornia.edu/wp-content/uploads/2019/03/Cortes_Research.pdf.

12. A few jurisdictions ban discrimination based on political affiliation, but this prohibition refers to affiliation with a party—not expression. See, e.g., D.C. Code § 2-1402.11.

13. See also Garrett Epps, "Free Speech Isn't Free," *The Atlantic*, February 7, 2014, https://www.theatlantic.com/politics/archive/2014/02/free-speech-isnt-free/283672/.

Does the First Amendment Apply to My School?

The First Amendment sets limits on government power. Although its text reads "Congress shall make no law," the First Amendment's protections apply to all levels and branches of government,[14] and to policies and regulations in addition to laws. For example, if a state university punishes a student for speaking in support of a political candidate, they have likely violated her First Amendment right to free speech, though neither Congress nor a "law" was involved. Public colleges and universities are considered government actors when it comes to First Amendment speech rights. If you attend a public institution, the First Amendment protects your expressive freedom on campus and limits your school's authority to censor or punish constitutionally protected expression.

The courts have repeatedly confirmed that speech, expression, and association rights on college campuses must be protected. In the mid-twentieth century, when legislatures sought to punish professors' and students' political activity—including anti-war protests, civil rights organizing, and scholarship—the courts ruled that these actions violated the First Amendment.[15]

14. "The Fourteenth Amendment and Incorporation," Bill of Rights Institute, https://billofrightsinstitute.org/essays/the-fourteenth-amendment-and-incorporation (accessed June 16, 2023).

15. See, e.g., *Healy v. James*, 408 U.S. 169 (1972): "The precedents of this Court leave no room for the view that, because of the acknowledged need for order, First Amendment protections should apply with less force on college campuses than in the community at large." To learn more about the history of free expression and

Wait a Minute! My Public High School Limited My Speech Rights! What's Up with That?

The Supreme Court famously ruled that students don't "shed their constitutional rights to freedom of speech or expression at the schoolhouse gate." This quotation from *Tinker v. Des Moines Independent School District* is often cited for the proposition that American public-school students have robust rights to free expression. In *Tinker,* the Court ruled that a school could not suspend students for wearing armbands to protest the Vietnam War. Mary Beth Tinker, one of the students whose rights the Supreme Court recognized, continues to be an activist and spokesperson for students' free speech rights. She is an inspiring speaker with a great story to tell about how one person's activism can make a difference. Unfortunately, I don't think her story paints an accurate picture of the state of expressive freedom in US schools. I would say Joseph Frederick's experience is sadly more typical.

The 2007 decision *Morse v. Frederick* is either comical or ominous, depending upon your perspective. Frederick was suspended for displaying a banner that said "Bong Hits 4 Jesus" during the Olympic torch relay, which he was attending as a school-supervised activity. Though Frederick stated that his sign was nonsense and that he had only wanted to get on television, the school principal argued that the sign promoted

---

association on campus, see Erwin Chemerinsky and Howard Gillman, *Free Speech on Campus* (New Haven, CT: Yale University Press, 2017).

illegal drug use. The Court concluded that this was a reasonable interpretation and upheld the suspension. The majority opinion by Chief Justice John Roberts, joined by two other justices who remain on the Court as of this writing (Clarence Thomas and Samuel Alito), indicates that students' speech rights at school (or at school-related activities) are less extensive than speech rights outside of school.

Regardless of what you think of Frederick's "Bong Hits 4 Jesus" stunt, *Morse v. Frederick* contains at least three important legal conclusions that should be of concern to those who support students' rights. First, although in First Amendment cases outside of K-12 education courts will examine the speaker's intent, school administrators may punish or censor speech without regard to the student's intent. Second, administrators have wide latitude to determine what a reasonable interpretation of the expression would be. And third, school administrators hold some power to punish speech that takes place off campus.[16]

As a result of the Court's rulings in speech cases like *Morse v. Frederick*, primary and secondary schools can limit students' speech and expression, including through punishments such as detention, suspension, and loss of access to opportunities and activities. Public school students' rights are an evolving area of law—with questions remaining about

16. In its 2021 decision in *Mahanoy Area School District, Petitioner v. B. L*, 594 U.S. 210 (2021), the Court ruled in favor of a student who had been disciplined for a profane post on Snapchat. Although the Court sided with the student in that case, it left open the possibility that schools could discipline students for social media or other off-campus speech—such as if it included threats or harassment.

how much authority schools may exert over off-campus expression.[17] Tinker's core holding—that nondisruptive student political expression is protected—remains an important one. It is likely that when future cases come before the Court, activity that reflects civic engagement—such as political activism—will receive greater First Amendment protection than speech that is merely playful, as in *Morse v. Frederick*.

In its 2021 decision in *Mahanoy Area School District v. BL*, the Court ruled in favor of a student who had been disciplined for a social post that said "F*ck cheer," referring to her disappointment with the school's cheerleading team.[18] Note that although this speech was profane, it was a critique of school policies and arguably core political speech. Although this student won her case, the Court declined to rule that schools can never punish off-campus speech.

While it is true that *Tinker* and *Mahanoy* were victories for students' rights, the Court's rulings left school administrators with an enormous amount of latitude to punish expression and expressive conduct that administrators believe might substantially disrupt school discipline or decorum. In Frederick's case, the Supreme Court made clear that school administrators get to decide whether speech will cause a "substantial disruption" and punish some speech that would be protected in the public square (or on college campuses).

17. See *Mahanoy Area School District, Petitioner v. B. L.*

18. *Mahanoy Area School District, Petitioner v. B. L.*

Primary and secondary school students are also subjected to dress and appearance codes that limit their individual expression. These codes, which are disproportionately enforced against girls and particularly affect Black girls,[19] sometimes overlap with limitations on student expression. For example, many school districts prohibit students from wearing clothing that depicts alcohol or drugs. And in an interesting twist on *Morse v. Frederick*, where the Supreme Court upheld a suspension for a message that could be interpreted as promoting drug use, one court upheld a school's decision to suspend a student for wearing a shirt with the "vulgar" anti-drug message "drugs suck."[20]

Many school districts also maintain restrictions on hairstyles, including some that ban culturally specific hairstyles such as dreadlocks. Others create gender-specific restrictions on apparel or appearance, such as requiring boys to have short hair or prohibiting girls from wearing "revealing" or "distracting" clothing. Some students and groups have successfully challenged dress codes that perpetuate gender stereotypes, and students' rights advocates continue to press for fairer dress codes. But dress codes that go far beyond the standards of modesty required to enter stores, restaurants, and other public spaces remain the norm for many students nationwide.

19. "Dress Coded: Black Girls, Bodies, and Bias in D.C. Schools," National Women's Law Center, April 24, 2018, https://nwlc.org/resource/dresscoded/.

20. See *Broussard By Lord v. School Bd. of City of Norfolk*, 801 F. Supp. 1526 (E.D. Va. 1992).

Why Does This Matter for College Students?

By the time they enter college, most US students have spent over twelve years in educational environments where personal expression is heavily regulated. From an early age, many students are told to report unkind speech to authority figures and are advised that excluding classmates is a kind of bullying (where outside of school, the choice of who we associate with is itself a constitutionally protected freedom). This makes some sense in that primary schools are a place for young children to learn how to be kind and respectful community members, and where teachers and administrators act *in loco parentis*—in the role of a parent, helping to preserve peace and safety and supporting students' emotional well-being. But it is different from higher education, where students are considered adults and where the balance between expressive freedom and school order and decorum shifts.

It is no wonder, then, that many college students are surprised to learn what a hands-off approach their schools will take to expression—including disrespectful or hateful expression. It is understandable that students have internalized the idea that a wide variety of speech can be punished. In May of their senior year, students can lose access to graduation privileges for a hairstyle.[21] Three months later, at college, it's a

21. Sascha Cordner, "Houston-Area Teen Inspires Texas Lawmakers to Tackle Hair Discrimination," Houston Public Media, February 7, 2020, https://www.houstonpublicmedia.org/articles/news/2020/02/07/360075/houston-area-teen-spurs-texas-lawmakers-to-file-bill-to-prevent-black-hair-discrimination/.

whole new set of rules—and often, students are not even told how the rules have changed.

The mindset that administrators and faculty can regulate and punish expression is baked into our education for years. Shifting from that mindset to the college discourse mindset is important, just like learning college-level writing skills or time management.

Private Colleges and Universities: Voluntary First Amendment–like Protections

Private institutions are more free than public ones to set limits on expression. In fact, private entities—including colleges and universities—have certain First Amendment rights of their own.[22] Because of their roles expanding and challenging previously understood ideas and teaching adult learners to think critically, universities have a special interest in protecting expressive freedom even when they have the institutional power to limit speech that some community members would find offensive.

Many private universities explicitly adopt policies on expressive freedom and dissent that track the First Amendment or

22. Universities that accept government funds might be subjected to First Amendment–like requirements, and some states have enacted laws requiring private universities to abide by the First Amendment. See: "The Basics: The First Amendment," PEN America, https://campusfreespeechguide.pen.org/the-law/the-basics/ (accessed June 16, 2023).

come close to it. For example, in 2015 the University of Chicago released a statement affirming that expressive freedom is central to the mission of the university. It reads, in relevant part:

> In a word, the University's fundamental commitment is to the principle that debate or deliberation may not be suppressed because the ideas put forth are thought by some or even by most members of the University community to be offensive, unwise, immoral, or wrong-headed. It is for the individual members of the University community, not for the University as an institution, to make those judgments for themselves, and to act on those judgments not by seeking to suppress speech, but by openly and vigorously contesting the ideas that they oppose.[23]

Dozens of private universities have adopted this statement or something similar. Many more include freedom of expression and freedom of inquiry within their mission statements. For example, the university where I teach includes "free inquiry and seeking truth" in its values statement.[24]

Check your university's mission statement, conduct code, and faculty and staff manuals for policies on inquiry, expression, and dissent. These policies will help you understand how your institution will address invited guest speakers, protests, and expressive activity like chalking and posting flyers.

23. "Report of the Committee on Freedom of Expression," University of Chicago, https://provost.uchicago.edu/sites/default/files/documents/reports/FOECommitteeReport.pdf (accessed June 16, 2023).

24. "American University's Mission," American University, https://www.american.edu/about/mission.cfm (accessed June 16, 2023).

The First Amendment and free expression policy statements. How do they affect expression on campus?

- Guest speakers. The university will not prevent clubs or departments from inviting speakers simply because they have made controversial or derogatory statements.
- Expression outside the classroom, such as on the campus quadrangle or outdoor gathering spaces. Signs, placards, art, student journalism, expressive clothing, and speech will not be censored or punished based on viewpoint.
- Faculty and student research and publication. Community members' choice of what to study or publish will not be censored or punished based on viewpoint.[25]
- Freedom from compelled speech. A public institution may not require you to express a viewpoint, such as by saluting the flag or agreeing with a school statement of policies. It can require you to abide by codes of conduct.
- Dissent, protest, and counterspeech. Student protests that do not materially interfere with the university's functioning are protected. Time, place, and manner restrictions can apply.

Even at public universities or private schools that adopt a First Amendment–like policy, the right to free expression is not unlimited. But the extent and nature of protected speech and

25. But ethical rules regarding research will apply. To learn more about research on human subjects, see your school's institutional review board (IRB) website, or see Michael White, "Why Human Subjects Research Protection Is Important," *The Ochsner Journal* 20, no. 1 (Spring 2020): 16–33.

expression on your campus—and the institution's ability or willingness to limit some expression—will vary.

Check your comprehension:

Which of these actions constitutes compelled speech in violation of the First Amendment?

- The marching band at a public university plays "The Star-Spangled Banner" at a college football game.
- A university's website says, "We are fortunate to live in the greatest country on Earth."
- A public university requires students to put their hand over their heart during the national anthem. Failure to do so violates the student conduct code, and infractions appear on the final transcript.
- At a private university, incoming students must take a pledge to uphold the values of truth, inclusiveness, and kindness.[26]

Private Colleges That Restrict Expression

Some private colleges establish limitations on speech beyond those that would be permissible at public institutions. Regulations might include:

26. The first two are examples of speech by the institution or its representatives. The third constitutes *compelled* speech. A public institution enforcing this rule violates the First Amendment, but a private institution could establish and enforce a conduct rule like this. The fourth is an example of a permissible regulation at a private school.

- Defining harassment more broadly than federal and state civil rights laws do, to include insulting and degrading language or slurs.
- Content-specific and restrictive policies and procedures for posting materials on campus (for example, requiring student groups to clear their posted materials with an administrator and prohibiting some content).
- Procedures and policies for responding to incidents when students or others use hateful language that would be protected speech at a public institution.
- Some religiously affiliated colleges and universities require students to affirm their faith or otherwise commit to a code of belief or conduct or abstain from using profanity.[27]
- Some private schools require students to attend chapel or convocation, including with prayer or invited speakers.[28]

These policies are often found in student codes of conduct and are generally available on institutions' websites. There are databases of policies where you can search for your own college or for colleges you might consider attending.[29]

27. For example, students at Brigham Young University agree not to use vulgar language and agree to attend church if they are members. "Church Educational System Honor Code," Brigham Young University, https://policy.byu.edu/view/church-educational-system-honor-code (accessed June 16, 2023).

28. "Convocation FAQ," Liberty University, https://www.liberty.edu/osd/lu-stages/convocation/faq/ (accessed June 16, 2023).

29. See, e.g., the Foundation for Individual Rights and Expression (FIRE), https://rankings.thefire.org/rank. To learn about campus policies, click on "speech codes." For information about how to use the database to find speech policies, see https://www.thefire.org/research-learn/using-fires-spotlight-database.

Student journalism can provide an excellent window on the extent of expressive freedom on a campus. If you are interested in learning about campus climate, read student newspapers and learn whether the school administration exercises any editorial control over them. A free press is a tool for holding authority figures and institutions accountable, including on college campuses.

What Kind of Speech Is Protected?

> "Whatever differences may exist about interpretations of the First Amendment, there is practically universal agreement that a major purpose of that amendment was to protect the free discussion of governmental affairs. This, of course, includes discussions of candidates, structures and forms of government, the manner in which government is operated or should be operated, and all such matters relating to political processes."[30]

This passage introduces us to an idea that lawyers and courts call "core political speech." This is speech that involves advocacy for political change; argues for or against candidates; critiques government officials, structures, or institutions; and challenges social conditions and practices, political positions, or prevailing ideas. In short, core political speech is what a tyrant would ban to secure absolute power. It is the engine of democratic society and of movements for social justice. Restrictions on core political speech are unlikely to survive constitutional challenges.

30. *Mills v. Alabama*, 384 U. S. 214 (1966), ruling that an Alabama law banning election-day editorials urging voters to vote a particular way violated the First Amendment.

We can see this when we consider public schools, where officials have more latitude than elsewhere to limit expressive freedom. Recall that the speech protected in *Tinker* was a critique of the war in Vietnam. "Bong Hits 4 Jesus," by contrast, was a stunt to grab attention. That core political speech would receive greater protection is consistent with both the purpose of the First Amendment and the role that schools themselves play in preparing students for life in a democracy. The Supreme Court has observed "that they are educating the young for citizenship is reason for scrupulous protection of Constitutional freedoms of the individual, if we are not to strangle the free mind at its source and teach youth to discount important principles of our government as mere platitudes."[31] However, regulating the kind of speech that would be protected in the public square is arguably counterproductive to the goal of preparing students for a democracy (or even for college).

Though it's useful to remember the First Amendment's purpose of guaranteeing freedom of dissent and self-governance in a democratic society, we must also remember that expressive freedom is not limited to political speech, or even to productive or true speech. Expression that is unkind, vulgar, or that offends community members is protected. Recall the case of *Texas v. Johnson*, where the Court struck down a flag desecration law. The very fact that burning a US flag was so shocking to many demonstrated its expressive power as political speech. Because expressive freedom is a protective measure against tyranny, it has long been used to protect unpopular

31. *West Virginia Bd. of Ed. v. Barnette*, 319 U.S. 624 (1943).

ideas and expression—from socialism and racial integration to flag burning—from being drowned out.

"Hate Speech" Is Not Protected, Is It?

Short answer: it is protected.

"Core political speech" sounds like lofty stuff. But outside of K-12 schools (which can punish profane or vulgar speech[32] or hateful speech),[33] speech need not be political or important to be protected. It can be vulgar, coarse, insulting, cruel, hateful, hurtful, or even false. Simply saying hateful things or being a member of hateful groups (such as the American Nazi Party or the Ku Klux Klan) does not remove someone from the protections of the First Amendment. Emotional harm alone does not convert protected expression into unprotected conduct.

Take the case of *Snyder v. Phelps*,[34] in which the Supreme Court ruled 8–1 in favor of the Westboro Baptist Church (WBC). WBC had picketed a US marine's funeral, carrying signs that read "god hates (slur meaning gay men)" and "thank god for dead soldiers." The Court ruled that WBC could not be held civilly liable[35] for demonstrating in a public place about a matter of public concern—regardless of how hateful the speech was.

Snyder v. Phelps was not the first decision to protect hateful speech. Courts have also upheld the rights of Nazis to march in

32. *Bethel School Dist. No. 403 v. Fraser*, 478 U.S. 675, (1986).

33. David Wheeler, "Do Students Still Have Free Speech in School?" *The Atlantic*, April 7, 2014, https://www.theatlantic.com/education/archive/2014/04/do-students-still-have-free-speech-in-school/360266/.

34. *Snyder v. Phelps*, 562 U.S. 443 (2011).

35. *Snyder v. Phelps*.

a town with a population of holocaust survivors.[36] In *Brandenburg v. Ohio*,[37] the Court ruled in favor of a Ku Klux Klan leader who was prosecuted under a state law that was traceable to the anti-Communist fervor of the early twentieth century. The state had argued that the KKK's marching was likely to cause a violent disturbance. The Court concluded that the mere potential for violent reactions was not a sufficient reason to abridge expressive freedom. Instead, it ruled that only speech that is (a) directed at inciting or producing "imminent lawless action" and (b) likely to incite such action may be punished.

In determining whether speech crosses the line from protected political speech to incitement, courts still apply the *Brandenburg* test. It's important to note that unlike in school speech cases, where administrators are free to disregard the speaker's intent (like Joseph Frederick's intention to get on TV), the *Brandenburg* test requires a showing that the speaker intended to incite imminent lawless action.

Incitement is an extremely narrow exception to the First Amendment's protections. When it comes to protecting the right to speak, the Court has protected even the most vehemently anti-freedom speakers. When considering whether speech is somehow exempt from First Amendment protection, *Brandenburg* can help remind you that the most hateful speech can be constitutionally protected.

The fact that the First Amendment protects speech by domestic terrorist groups like the KKK serves as a reminder never to mistake the burdens of free expression for its benefits. The

36. See *Village of Skokie v. Nat'l Socialist Party of America*, 69 Ill. 2d 605 (1978).
37. *Brandenburg v. Ohio*, 395 US 444 (1969).

Court's rulings do not mean that the KKK or the WBC have something valuable to say, nor that if we invite them to our campuses to denigrate people, our community will be better off. The question whether speech is protected and the question whether it belongs in a decent society are two entirely separate questions. And that is why this book doesn't end on page X.

Expressions such as burning a cross are also protected unless the government also proves the expression was made with an intent to intimidate someone.[38] As I will cover below in the section on free speech exceptions, threatening or intimidating another person is not protected speech. But the Court has ruled that displaying a symbol alone is not a threat. The fact that a viewer might feel outraged—or even threatened—by expression is not enough to create a First Amendment exception. The law distinguishes between hateful expression (protected) and unprotected *conduct* such as harassment or threat. Many disputes over expression on campus require us to understand the difference between protected expression and unprotected conduct.

Big Idea: Expression can be protected even if onlookers find it upsetting. For example, a racial justice march through a residential area would be protected even if people in the neighborhood were unaccustomed to protests and felt upset that nonresidents were present, so long as the march didn't violate laws unrelated to expression (such traffic or noise ordinances).

38. See *RAV v. St. Paul*, 505 U.S. 377 (1992), holding that an ordinance banning displays of certain symbols banned protected speech based only on content; and *Virginia v. Black*, 538 U.S. 343 (2003), holding that while the state may ban cross burning *with intent to intimidate*, the act of burning a cross cannot be criminalized absent a showing of intent to intimidate.

What about "Hate Speech"?

"Hate speech" is defined as pejorative language with reference to a person or group based on who they are.[39] For example, describing a religious or ethnic minority group as inferior, comparing them to disease or contagion; attributing undesirable characteristics (uncleanliness, criminality) to people; or describing a group as predatory are all examples of what scholars of extremism and intergroup conflict term hate speech. Some people have defined certain strains of hateful speech as "dangerous" speech, noting that it can create the political and social conditions that lead to persecution or genocide.[40] This definition is useful in understanding conditions in society so that we may counter them through education and solidarity with targeted groups. But "hate speech" is not a legally distinct category of speech that is exempt from First Amendment protection.

Hate Crimes and Hate Speech Are Not the Same

A federal law and the laws of most[41] states criminalize acts of violence motivated by the victim's actual or perceived characteristics. Hate crimes statutes do not criminalize speech or thought. They create a classification of crimes motivated by

39. "What Is Hate Speech?" United Nations, https://www.un.org/en/hate-speech/understanding-hate-speech/what-is-hate-speech (accessed June 16, 2023).

40. "Dangerous Speech: A Practical Guide," The Dangerous Speech Project, April 19, 2021, https://dangerousspeech.org/guide/.

41. "Laws and Policies: Hate Crimes," US Department of Justice, updated May 9, 2022, https://www.justice.gov/hatecrimes/laws-and-policies.

antipathy toward a group.[42] In a hate crime prosecution the accused person's speech and expression can be used as evidence of their motive, but are not themselves criminal.

For example, marching with neo-Nazis is a protected form of association, and carrying a sign that reads "Jews will not replace us" is a form of protected expression. But if a defendant is charged with a hate crime—assaulting someone because the victim is Jewish—evidence of his speech and conduct could be used to show that this was in fact a bias-motivated crime, and not an ordinary fist fight.

Surveys[43] show that many students believe that "hate speech" is not "free speech." This view, though legally inaccurate, is widespread and not limited to students. Many Americans believe that hate speech is a distinct category of unprotected speech.[44]

This should not be surprising. Most of us spend the bulk of our time in contexts where hateful expression is not permitted. Families, schools, sports teams, faith communities, and workplaces can all provide disincentives, if not outright prohibitions, on the kind of expression at issue in *Snyder v. Phelps* or *Brandenburg v. Ohio*. Furthermore, most of us, upon learn-

42. See "The Matthew Shepard and James Byrd, Jr., Hate Crimes Prevention Act of 2009," US Department of Justice, updated October 18, 2018, https://www.justice.gov/crt/matthew-shepard-and-james-byrd-jr-hate-crimes-prevention-act-2009-0; hate crimes laws are applied equally regardless of the perpetrator's or the victim's identity. For example, if a woman committed a crime motivated by hatred toward men, it could be prosecuted as a hate crime.

43. John Villasenor, "Views Among College Students Regarding the First Amendment: Results from a New Survey," Brookings, September 18, 2017, https://www.brookings.edu/blog/fixgov/2017/09/18/views-among-college-students-regarding-the-first-amendment-results-from-a-new-survey/.

44. "Speech: The First Amendment: Where America Stands," Freedom Forum, https://survey.freedomforum.org/speech/ (accessed June 16, 2023).

ing that Nazi propaganda is constitutionally protected, still do not want to spread it. This fact is not always taught in high schools, and a relevant course is not a core requirement even for most college majors.

The broadly held misconception that "hate speech" is not protected could be a source of conflict on campuses. Imagine you attend a state university bound by the First Amendment not to censor speech based on viewpoint. A group like WBC comes to a publicly accessible part of campus carrying signs condemning LGBTQ people and others. Their message is hateful to many members of the community, but the administration does not attempt to remove the speakers. For students who believe that the university had the power to exclude these speakers (it does not), this incident could be doubly painful: they are confronted both with a message of hatred and with the impression that their university does not care.

Understanding that hate speech is protected enables students to see the university's actions (or inaction) in a different light.[45] Understanding that the school cannot censor hateful expression is not a perfect solution for those who would prefer to protect community members from being exposed to hate. But understanding what speech is protected also allows student activists and administrators to channel their energies into other responses, including counterspeech, education, and restorative discussions.

45. At a private university, students might perceive a voluntarily adopted free expression policy as an embrace or endorsement for hateful speech. It is important for schools to discuss why embracing expressive freedom is in their community's interest—and to understand that simply saying "this speech is protected" will not necessarily satisfy students who have concerns about hateful speech proliferating.

What This Means for Campus Speakers

There have been numerous clashes between students and administrations over guest speakers who are perceived to (or actually) espouse views that degrade community members. Some students have demanded that schools not provide a platform to such speakers. At a public university, this would constitute unconstitutional viewpoint discrimination—censoring speech based on the content of the message.

Although public universities cannot ban speakers based on viewpoint, they can exercise their own speech rights. College administrators can issue statements disavowing speakers whose message conflicts with the university's values or mission. They can also offer counterprogramming, provide education to rebut misinformation, and choose to allocate university resources consistent with their educational mission. For example, though a public university may not bar a notoriously antisemitic speaker from campus, they are not obligated to offer a course in Holocaust denial alongside their courses in Judaic studies and twentieth-century history.

I Get It, But It Seems Like the First Amendment Does Bad Things, Actually

When we consider cases like *Brandenburg* and *Phelps,* First Amendment protections appear costly. Why not try to regulate the most hateful expression? Although this book is not a piece of advocacy about what the law (or private policies) should be, it is still useful to lay out the reason why supporters of expressive freedom (like myself) do not support trying to craft carve-outs for hateful speech. Put simply, when we devise a limitation on freedom, we must consider how it would be enforced, and whether this authority could be used (or abused) to silence voices of justice or entrench inequality. Historically, restrictions on speech have been leveraged against civil rights advocates.[46]

If Hateful Expression Is Protected, How Can You Say Free Speech Is Not Unlimited?

No constitutional right is unlimited. One way to think about rights is that our own rights end where other people's rights begin. My freedom to swing my arm does not extend to hitting your face. My freedom to exercise my religion does not extend to human sacrifice. The following expression and expressive conduct are unprotected whether you are on a college campus or in a public square:

Incitement

Expression that intends to and has the effect of inciting imminent lawless action. Courts define this kind of speech very narrowly. It is not enough to say, "at some point, people are going to rise up and take back our country from (the disfavored

46. "Minorities Suffer the Most from Hate-Speech Laws," Spiked Online, December 14, 2018, https://www.spiked-online.com/2018/12/14/minorities-suffer-the-most-from-hate-speech-laws/.

group)." To be incitement (and thus not protected), the speech must encourage people to take action that violates the law: for example, telling a crowd to attack a specific person or storm a building, creating a danger of imminent unlawful action.

True Threat

A true threat conveys that a speaker means to "commit an act of unlawful violence."[47] To be a true threat, expression must be likely to convey the danger of immediate bodily harm, and the speaker must have some subjective understanding of their statements' threatening nature.[48] Intimidation is a category of threat and can include the use of threatened violence to coerce a target (for example, threatening violence to rob someone). Note that for the purpose of distinguishing between protected and unprotected speech, the concepts of violence and threat relate to bodily harm, not emotional harm. Although some disciplines outside of the law define the word "violence" to include structures of social injustice,[49] this definition does not apply in First Amendment law.

Defamation

False statements that injure the target's reputation are known as defamation. Truth is an absolute defense to defamation claims. This means that true speech that damages a person's

47. See *Virginia v. Black*, 538 U.S. 343 (2003).

48. See *Counterman v. Colorado*, 600 US __(2023) (slip opinion available at https://www.supremecourt.gov/opinions/22pdf/22-138_43j7.pdf).

49. See Paul E. Farmer, Bruce Nizeye, Sara Stulac, and Salmaan Keshavjee, "Structural Violence and Clinical Medicine," *PLOS Medicine* 3, no. 10 (2006): e449.

reputation is not considered defamatory. To be defamatory, a statement must also be *verifiably* false—a statement of fact, not opinion. Statements of opinion that are unkind but subjective—such as that someone is "unattractive" or "mean"—are not defamatory.

Harassment

Harassment is prohibited *conduct* that can include elements of speech. Federal and state civil rights laws that prohibit discrimination in educational activities also bar harassment.[50] Although the existence of hateful rhetoric can make a person feel that the campus is not welcoming, the presence of hateful speech on campus (for example, the presence of Adolph Hitler's *Mein Kampf* in the library; an invited guest speaker denigrating a religion; a professor publishing an op-ed criticizing or supporting abortion rights; or someone displaying any of these kinds of messages on posters they carry across the campus), without more, cannot constitute harassment. As a rule, you can tell the difference between protected speech and harassment by considering the following questions.

1. Is it targeted?

Recall that the First Amendment protects hateful expression. Marchers who chant "Jews will not replace us" spread a hateful, white supremacist ideology, but that statement does not constitute incitement. Nor would a general statement about a

50. See Title VI of the Civil Rights Act of 1964, 42 U.S.C. 2000d -2000d-7 and Title IX of the Education Amendments of 1972, 20 U.S.C. §1681–1688.

group—not directed at a particular person—constitute harassment. But if the marchers went to a specific person's home, got their attention, and shouted you will not replace us, that speech would be targeted, and could be harassment.

2. Is it severe, pervasive, and unwelcome?

Even targeted speech is not harassment unless it is particularly egregious (for example, threatening consequences such as job loss) or pervasive—including interaction that persists after the target expresses that it is unwelcome. When someone says they don't wish to engage in conversation, have further contact, or remain on the topic at hand, later efforts to continue the conversation could be harassing. When a student or employee tells someone in authority—such as a supervisor or dean—that they have been targeted by unwelcome speech and conduct, the school or employer can be held responsible for failing to prevent further harassment.

3. Is it gratuitous?

Sometimes classroom or workplace discussion relates to sensitive topics. For example, an employer might have to ask a worker about their marital status to enroll their dependents in health insurance. Prying into a worker's personal life without a work-related reason could be harassment if it is repeated and unwelcome. A class might discuss violent and hateful episodes from history. However, spontaneously asking a Jewish classmate if anyone in their family had been killed in the Holocaust and continuing with the subject after a request to stop, could be harassment.

Check for comprehension—let's apply the rule:

1. A student group invites a speaker to present her research about abusive behavior by Catholic priests. The speaker has a history of criticizing the Catholic Church (and Catholicism itself). Many people believe the speaker harbors anti-Catholic bias. Does the campus event constitute harassment based on religion?
2. In a class discussion about abortion policy, a male student stated that they support laws limiting abortion. In response, another student observed that abortion restrictions would not affect that student personally. The male student responded that the full class was not respecting his viewpoints as a Christian. In response, another student encouraged him not to "make this all about you." Does this classroom dialogue include harassment based on sex or religion?[51]

Viewpoint Neutrality and Content Discrimination

Although expressive freedom is not unlimited, government regulations on speech must be viewpoint neutral. Viewpoint and content discrimination—regulations that reflect the

51. Answer: (1) No. The speech is expression, not harassment. (2) No. Although in this case, all parties might want to consider (and the professor might request) not making "you" statements or personalizing the dispute, this does not amount to harassment. If the students repeatedly took steps to exclude one student from speaking or participating based on their sex, this could rise to harassment. Note that although views on abortion are often informed by religious belief, disagreeing with a classmate's views on abortion does not necessarily constitute denigrating their religious belief.

government taking sides—are most likely to run afoul of the First Amendment (or similar voluntary protections for expression).

By contrast, viewpoint-neutral, time, place, and manner restrictions are generally acceptable. If a school bans all amplified speech on the main quad after 10 P.M., this is a viewpoint-neutral restriction even if it incidentally affects protests. On the other hand, if a university passed a regulation barring amplified speeches after 10 P.M. but permitting the marching band to play after sporting events, we might infer they are suppressing protest—not protecting students' quiet study time. These examples illustrate the line between permissible and impermissible regulations:

- A public university may prohibit students from displaying signs in windows that are designated fire escape routes, but it may not ban campaign signs while permitting sports banners and US flags.
- A university with a strong free expression policy may (and must) protect students from harassment, including severe and pervasive insults targeted at a specific student. But it will not block a student group from inviting a guest speaker who has made racist statements.

Remember: the fact that expression is protected from official censorship or punishment does not mean that it meets the standards applicable to academic work.

Speech in the Classroom: From "Free Speech" to Speech with Standards

Viewpoint and content neutrality is more complicated in college courses than in many other contexts because academic speech is subject to standards that speech in the public square is not. Citizens, political candidates, and elected officials are free to make unsupported claims. By contrast, if you do so in a college course you will likely be marked down or asked to submit a rewrite.

It is critical to use accurate terminology when describing viewpoint neutrality in our polarized time. In particular, viewpoint neutrality and bipartisanship are not the same thing (in fact, they could contradict one another). "Bipartisan" refers to legislation or other measures created with input or approval from members of both major US political parties. "Nonpartisan" means unaffiliated with a political party. A viewpoint-neutral college policy or practice will be nonpartisan, not bipartisan.

Is Viewpoint Discrimination Permissible in Classrooms?

No, and yes.

Freedom to learn and to express ideas without regard to partisan or ideological orientation is essential in college. This language comes from the class policies documents I share with my students each semester:

- This course will assess your knowledge of the material; higher-order engagement with course concepts; persuasive communication; use of evidence to construct reasoned and logical arguments; improvement; engagement with peers' and instructor's ideas and questions; bravery; and respectful and thought-provoking contributions to the learning community.

- This course will not assess: native English language proficiency or dialect; disability or neurodiversity; prior knowledge or preformed opinions; political belief or expression; identity; access to professional and personal networks; trauma history; or any other factor unrelated to work in our course.
- College is a time to engage with challenging ideas and material. We benefit from our diverse learning community. All voices are welcome. You are responsible for defending your arguments with case law and/or other verifiable evidence. We discuss ideas, not talking points or individuals' worth.

If you ask professors whether they agree on the values of free expression and viewpoint neutrality expressed here, the overwhelming majority will say yes.[52] We want learning communities where students participate actively and where texts and ideas are subjected to intensive scrutiny, comparison, and analysis. Research has not found evidence that professors grade students based on ideology or partisanship.[53]

52. There would probably be a great deal of disagreement about whether native language proficiency or dialect should affect grades. A writing or public speaking course, for example, could be graded in part on demonstrating such proficiency.

53. Steven Johnson, "Is Political Bias in Grading a Myth?" *The Chronicle of Higher Education*, February 13, 2019, https://www.chronicle.com/article/is-political-bias-in-grading-a-myth/.

And although ideologically liberal college faculty outnumber conservative ones, students who engage with faculty tend to moderate their own viewpoints.[54]

Nonetheless, surveys show that many students report being hesitant to speak up in class,[55] and that self-identified conservative students are more likely than self-identified liberals to report concealing their views.[56] What does this mean?

Although we professors engage with our students only in the context of our courses or programs, students understand themselves as members of a broader college community. And although I would like to believe that mastering the craft of legal analysis is every student's top priority, I know students have other things on their minds—including, significantly, their relationships with peers.

Surveys of student opinion can't tell us everything. For starters, they don't specify which opinions the students are suppressing. These surveys could be evidence of political self-censorship but might also reflect students trying to be kind,[57]

54. See Kyle Dodson, "The Effect of College on Social and Political Attitudes and Civic Participation," in *Professors and Their Politics*, ed. Neil Gross and Solon Simmons (Baltimore: Johns Hopkins University Press, 2014), 135–157.

55. "Free Expression on College Campuses," The Knight Foundation, May 2019, https://kf-site-production.s3.amazonaws.com/media_elements/files/000/000/351/original/Knight-CP-Report-FINAL.pdf.

56. Timothy J. Ryan, Andrew M. Engelhardt, Jennifer Larson, and Mark McNeilly, "Free Expression and Constructive Dialogue in the University of North Carolina System," Free Expression and Constructive Dialogue at the University of North Carolina, August 21, 2022, https://fecdsurveyreport.web.unc.edu/wp-content/uploads/sites/22160/2022/08/FECD_Report_8-21-22.pdf.

57. Elizabeth Niehaus, "Self-Censorship or Just Being Nice: Understanding College Students' Decisions About Classroom Speech," University of California

or hesitating to speak because they are uncertain how to communicate about sensitive topics without causing offense.[58]

What the surveys and op-eds have called "self-censorship," I consider at least three distinct categories of self-regulation:

- **Normative**: desirable self-regulation for classrooms; refraining from personal attacks; speaking only on relevant topics; offering claims supported by credible evidence.
- **Developmental**: self-regulation that reflects that students are still learning college speech rules and norms and developing the skills to communicate about new material in a new, diverse community.
- **Chilled speech**: students are suppressing well-reasoned lines of thought out of concern for the perceived consequences of disagreeing with their peers.

Normative self-censorship is not a problem; developmental self-censorship is a reason to keep practicing and learning college discourse—including the skills I'll share in the remainder of this book. Chilled speech, where present, is antithetical to the values of higher education. But it is important to distinguish it from the academic norms and rules of classroom speech that form a type of "content discrimination" that is distinct from viewpoint discrimination as First Amendment or academic freedom scholars understand it (or as partisan commentators describe it).

National Center for Free Speech and Civic Engagement, 2020–2021, https://freespeechcenter.universityofcalifornia.edu/fellows-20-21/niehaus-research/.

58. Lara Schwartz and Harsha Mudaliar, "Guest Post: Not So Fast on Campus Self-Censorship," Inside Higher Ed, January 30, 2022, https://www.insidehighered.com/blogs/just-visiting/guest-post-not-so-fast-campus-self-censorship.

A Self-Fulfilling Prophecy

Incidents where college students shut down speech have been the subject of intense national conversations. Newspaper editorial boards have claimed that an epidemic of "cancel culture" or "self-censorship" pervades college campuses. Regardless of whether it tells a true story, this narrative about higher education seems to be affecting what happens in classrooms. I have seen firsthand that some students hold pessimistic views of college before they even arrive on campus.

In all my courses, students do a pre-course survey in which they share their goals, concerns, and questions about the class. I noticed starting in about 2017 that many first-semester students, including liberal students, stated that they expected conservative viewpoints to be suppressed. I eventually started asking them where they got that idea: Had they heard of someone at American University who was shouted down? Had they heard that professors shut down disagreement?

They had not.

It was *a known fact* that the school is liberal (itself a vague term), and that on campuses today, a form of groupthink prevents people from speaking freely. Students across the political spectrum have consistently told me they would prefer an environment where ideas can be shared without regard to party or ideology. They say they want respectful conversation and to understand opposing views. This is consistent with surveys of college students nationwide.[59]

59. "College Student Views on Free Expression and Campus Speech 2022: A Look at Key Trends in Student Speech Views Since 2016," The Knight Foundation,

Students' perception of what college will be like can become a self-fulfilling prophecy. If students believe that college is not a place where ideas can be exchanged freely, they might choose not to engage in such an exchange of ideas. Thus, belief becomes reality—even though professors don't want it to happen.

And sometimes professors subtly (or not so subtly) discourage dialogue by making our own preferences clear, by generalizing our policy preferences as if they are shared by the whole class, and by not being explicit with our students that we welcome their disagreement. One of my student colleagues in the Project on Civil Discourse, a self-identified conservative woman who is a trained dialogue facilitator, has been enormously helpful in pointing out the ways a carelessly deployed comment can give the impression that there is only one way of thinking in a classroom.[60]

Academia Is Not a Viewpoint-Neutral Public Square

Classroom discussion and academic writing are both bound by standards and practices, some of which are specific to the discipline being studied (e.g., history or biology). Having completed twelve or more years of education before coming

January 2022, https://knightfoundation.org/wp-content/uploads/2022/01/KFX_College_2022.pdf.

60. Remarks by Anna Given, in Lara Schwartz, Keisuke Fujio, Anna Given, Chanelle Bonsu, and Sarah Marc Woeesner, "The Quiet Classroom: Recognizing and Responding to Student Hesitancy to Speak Up," panel presentation at the Ann Ferren Conference, American University, January 12, 2023, https://edspace.american.edu/afc/session-301/.

to college, you know that your oral and written expression is evaluated. By the time you enter college, students have internalized some standards of classroom discussion (respectfulness, relevance). These rules still apply in college. Some standards are worth discussing here because they are enforced more strictly in college or because for some students, they are not introduced until college.[61]

- Comments should reflect preparation and refer to assigned reading: in high school, volunteering one's personal opinion might be sufficient. Often, class time will be spent learning or explaining the material. In college classes, students are expected to complete assigned readings before class and refer to readings in class discussion.
  - *Why it matters*: You might find that if you offer a personal or political opinion that does not connect to the reading, the instructor will move on to another student or redirect you to the reading. This could feel like a critique of your politics, but it is an academic norm.
- Consider whether your claims are objective (provable) or subjective (matters of opinion): most of us are exposed to an enormous amount of opinion writing. Opinion writing (including social media) communicates personal perspectives and subjective judgments. Academic argumentation strives to be defensible by logic, reason, evidence, analysis, or other means.[62]

61. See Andrea Brenner and Lara Schwartz, *How to College*, 1st ed. (St. Martin's, 2019).

62. Students (and their professors) still explore and develop our opinions and preferences. The process of inquiry does not require us to pretend we are blank

Subjective claims	Provable claims
Cancel culture is insidious	Punishing speech deters people from expressing themselves
Separating families at the border is monstrous	Separating families at the border is a departure from prior practice

Students need to develop the skill of making provable claims and supporting them with evidence in class discussion and particularly in written work. In some circumstances, you might want to make a subjective claim based on your intuition or experience in order to explore a challenging text or topic. For example, the claim "this seems wrong to me" reflects that you have a concern about the text, but your thought process might not be that far along yet. Observations like this can be worth bringing into class discussion. Have a goal in mind and consider converting your observation to a question. For example: asking whether others have noticed contradictions in the text could lead to a more focused discussion than simply stating "this text is wrong."

- *Why it matters*: Many college writing assignments ask you to write a persuasive paper making and supporting an objective claim. If you write an opinion piece (abortion restrictions are bad; building a wall is good)

---

slates. Understanding the difference between subjective and objective claims can help us frame our dialogue. Subjective claims can lead us to productive and lovable questions, such as: *Why* do I prefer this policy or idea to another? Under what circumstances might I find this concept less troubling or more attractive?

you are unlikely to earn a high grade. Read your instructor's feedback: it can help you transform your opinion piece into a persuasive paper.

Test what you know:

Which of these are objective claims?

- The campus meal plan is literally the worst.
- Dollar for dollar, it would be cheaper to eat every meal at Panera than to buy the mandatory meal plan.
- Our campus has more cases of food poisoning per meal served than any other college in the state.
- Dining hall food makes my elementary school food look like *Top Chef*.[63]

- Use language with precision: by the time we arrive at college, people who grew up in the United States have also heard a lot of partisan or campaign-related communications, the object of which is to persuade voters to choose one side over the other. Generalizations about loosely defined terms or groups (liberals, conservatives, socialists, right-wingers) are a hallmark of political discourse. In academic spaces, this kind of communication fails to meet two related neutral (nonpartisan) standards—precision and verifiability.
    - *Why it matters*: If you make generalities about groups or use vague terms, you are likely to get negative

63. 2 and 3 are provable claims. 1 and 4 are subjective, and do not make reference to any measurable standard.

feedback regardless of whether your professor shares your partisan or policy preferences.

There are some other types of academic expression that are unprotected: plagiarism and academic integrity violations, for example. It's a good idea to find and review your college's academic integrity code if you haven't already.

Faculty have the authority (and responsibility) to maintain a classroom free of harassment. College faculty usually do not intervene in student interactions the way high school teachers do (and we do not have any connection with your home and family lives, unlike high school teachers who communicate with parents).[64] However, college faculty do act as stewards of class time: redirecting conversations back to course materials; enforcing standards of evidence; reminding students of community standards; correcting inaccurate statements; and attempting to ensure that all voices get equal time or at least access to equal time. If you're unsure how you are doing in class—for example, if you're concerned that your professor isn't calling on you as much as you'd like—go to office hours and ask.

Do the Rules Serve Order, Justice, Neither, or Both?

As scholars and learners, we may find some rules beneficial. For example, if I were to design an education system from the ground up, it would include a rule or norm about plagiarism.

64. Federal laws limit your school's authority to share information such as your grades and progress. "Family Educational Rights and Privacy Act (FERPA)," Electronic Privacy Information Center (EPIC), https://epic.org/family-educational-rights-and-privacy-act-ferpa/ (accessed June 16, 2023).

Other rules and norms might be simple matters of custom and might not serve a practical purpose. Understanding rules and norms is just the beginning. We can also evaluate and challenge rules and practices, from disciplinary standards and customs to laws and constitutions.

Norms and Civility: An Unspoken Code

College discourse also has unwritten norms. Some will be familiar from earlier in your education. For example, unless your professor specifies otherwise, it's a safe bet that profanity isn't welcome in the classroom. I like to draw attention to this norm because it's so commonly applied that you might not even notice it.

The fact is, categorizing certain words as profane (and forbidden) is what sociologists[65] would label a "construct." Unlike gravity and photosynthesis (rules of nature), a construct is human-made and can be quite specific to the context or society that made it. Considering this artificial rule can help shed light on our values about expression.

The late Comedian George Carlin did a routine about words you can't say on television.[66] These words are still not permitted on network television, but in the digital age, the practice of censoring them does not have the same cultural impact it once did. In fact, now that many of us can get instant access to content excluded from spaces like network TV and

65. See Peter L. Berger and Thomas Luckmann, *The Social Construction of Reality: A Treatise on the Sociology of Knowledge* (New York: Anchor Books, 1966).

66. The words are: sh!t, p!ss, f*ck, c*nt, c*cksucker, motherf*cker, and t!ts.

classrooms, such rules do not dictate *whether* most people are exposed to a word, but when, or how.

Still, the practice of identifying some words as profane can teach us about speech regulation and, in particular, the difference between speech rules that have communitarian purposes (such as kindness or inclusion) and ones related to tradition or propriety as socially constructed.

The words on Carlin's list are not, with the possible exception of the notorious "c-word," inherently unkind. All are proscribed on television, in contexts where children are present, and in many workplaces. In fact, if you get to say the words in class when discussing this book, that's a sign you are in college, not high school. Even in publications geared toward adults, these words are seldom printed. You might see them represented as "sh-t," "f—k," "(expletive)," or "explicit term for breasts." Much like the practice in some faith communities of writing "G-d" rather than "God," editorial care with the forbidden words signifies that these words are special and should be used sparingly.

What in the Actual F*ck?

It would be hard to argue that rules against profanity serve any of the purposes that are usually put forth to justify limiting speech. The norm against using profanity wasn't designed to promote justice or fairness. Most of the Seven Deadly Words are not inherently unkind. The so-called c-word is a misogynist slur in the United States (also a culture-specific construct; in England, you might hear someone refer to their cat as a c-word). That doesn't explain its presence on the list; we do not ban all misogynist language. You can refer to a woman as a hag, a nag, a witch, a crone, or any number of terms that signify female unworthiness without violating the profanity norm. Unlike slurs, these profane words don't insult individuals or create ingroups and outgroups.

Nor do they communicate inadequately. If you say a paper is a piece of sh*t, most people will know you mean it's very bad (but not why; it is a subjective assessment). In drama and comedy, profanity can add emotion and humor. Discouraging profanity seems to have no moral or practical basis, but most people in academic settings don't spend a lot of time criticizing the norm against profanity as a form of censorship. By contrast, there is an ongoing debate over whether banning racial slurs from the classroom is illiberal or unwise.[67]

I'm not encouraging you to use profanity in the classroom. I sometimes do and my students are welcome, but not obligated, to do so as well. I have the privilege of being able to set that norm in my courses. Another unspoken college norm is that professors decide many classroom rules, from whether you get to drop an F bomb to whether you get to eat or drink there.

I hope our critical examination of this norm inspires you to approach all policies—whether they appear benign, useful, or evil—with a mindset of inquiry and curiosity. I encourage you to consider ways in which apparently neutral rules and norms of academic and professional discourse can be counterproductive. The practice of marking students down for commu-

67. Randall L. Kennedy, "Who Can Say '—'? And Other Considerations," *Journal of Blacks in Higher Education* 26 (Winter 1999–2000): pp. 89–96.

nicating in a dialect other than standard academic English is one example I like to explore in class discussions.

Liberalism: An Intellectual Norm

Liberalism is another unspoken norm of higher education in the United States. This kind of liberalism doesn't refer to the political left; it means the mindset that civil liberties and expressive freedom are core values of a democratic society. A liberal response to hurtful or untrue speech is more speech or education, which will supposedly result in the superior ideas winning out. Speech in a liberal society has thus been called a "marketplace of ideas." Critiques of liberalism and of the "marketplace of ideas" abound. Markets sometimes produce junk. When some people have more power in the "market" of ideas, the best ideas can potentially get lost.

The idea that academic freedom and expressive freedom are core values of higher education—as expressed in mission statements, codes of conduct, and policies on free expression and dissent—is derived from the assumption that higher education is a fundamentally liberal enterprise, and that policies or practices that depart from this tradition and norm are inherently repugnant to the mission higher of education. This value is also widely held among journalists, politicians, and many US voters, and could explain why, even though our Constitution provides private universities the freedom to regulate speech, most higher education leaders would find that unacceptable.

Liberalism is also connected to the concept of civility, which dictates that participants in a dialogue observe community norms relating to noise, language, and equal access to educational spaces. Civility is sometimes used interchangeably with politeness. When we define civility this way, cool rationality and calm are preferable to high emotion and anger. But the term "civility" comes from the same common root as citizenship (*civilitas*).

The norm of liberalism could explain why campus speech has become a culture war issue in ways that other college concerns have not. Shouting down a speaker is said to be uncivil and illiberal. This act transgresses explicit community rules about disrupting programming, but that does not explain why disputes about guest speakers have captured so much media attention or brought so much criticism to students. After all, college campuses are home to a great deal of disruptive and even illegal behavior. When students riot after a big game or athletic championship, school operations can be disrupted, property destroyed, and people injured. Alcohol use—particularly when combined with hazing rituals—can disrupt education. College graduation rates nationwide are quite low,[68] and the high cost of education is one of the major barriers to completion.[69] But if you open your newspaper or browser and read about threats to higher education, you will find far more attention paid to the illiberal impulses of many

68. Michael Itzkowitz, "The State of American Higher Education Outcomes," Third Way, July 18, 2017, https://www.thirdway.org/report/the-state-of-american-higher-education-outcomes.

69. Jacob Roble, "Poverty Fact Sheet: Financial Barriers to College Completion," Morgridge Center for Public Service Institute for Research on Poverty, 2017, https://www.irp.wisc.edu/publications/factsheets/pdfs/FactSheet12-CollegeBarriers.pdf.

college students than to alcohol abuse, debt, food insecurity, racism, and interpersonal violence.

Outcry about some students' attempts to shut down controversial speakers reflects a sense that this behavior—unlike binge drinking or students having to work multiple jobs to secure their education—is inherently repugnant to what college education is all about. There is some truth to this assessment. I believe that trolling is also contrary to the mission of higher education. Yet our system of free expression protects speech that is itself inimical to the pursuit of knowledge in an academic community—including speech that misinforms, alienates, and excludes. This is why understanding the rules is not enough. The practice of dialogue requires generous listening and productive communication. The coming chapters will show you how to build and use these skills in classroom discussions, writing, and in your communities.

Discussion Questions and Classroom Exercises for Chapter 3

- Consider your high school's dress code and the regulations, if any, about expression and speech. What was their stated purpose? What messages did they send about the kind of people the school wanted you to become? What alternative would you propose? If you did not recall or did not see a written code, consider any instances where students were disciplined or asked to change their speech, dress, or expression.
- Since *Morse v. Frederick* was decided, numerous states and jurisdictions have decriminalized cannabis. Would

the case come out differently today, when advocating for marijuana legalization is a popular political movement? Under what circumstances would the speech be protected?

- When you think of freedom of expression, do you think of particular social movements, political parties, or ideologies? Is expressive freedom a value that you believe helps someone like you? If so, why? If not, why not?
- Under what circumstances should a university make an institutional statement about matters of public concern? How do such statements affect community members who disagree? How might an institution's silence affect community members?
- Normative self-censorship, developmental self-censorship, and chilled speech.
  - How would you define desirable (*normative*) self-censorship (e.g., not telling a classmate you believe they are unintelligent)? Do you practice normative self-censorship? Are there circumstances when it's hard to know whether keeping quiet is a good idea (e.g., if you are concerned about a friend's smoking but they haven't asked your opinion)?
  - Are there times when it is hard to express yourself because you don't know the subject matter well enough, because you are unsure of the correct vocabulary to use, or some other reason related to where you are in the learning process (*developmental self-censorship*)? How should our class handle attempts to discuss challenging issues where some or many class members don't yet have the vocabulary or knowledge

they wish they had? What would you need in order to build your skills in these areas? How can the class support one another in making these efforts? Do we want a degree of confidentiality? How do we plan to give and receive constructive criticism?
   - Do you want to hear opposing viewpoints about topics that matter to you? Why or why not? Are there any topics where you don't think you could engage in principled disagreement in class? What are some good reasons to hear and engage with differing perspectives? If there are some disagreements worth having, even when the positions are unpopular, what can we do as a class to open this space for the exchange of such ideas?
- Consider the unspoken norms of behavior and speech that apply in academic and other settings. What rules do faculty set? Which ones do students set (e.g., students typically set norms for dress)? Do these unspoken rules apply to all community members equally? How are the rules enforced? Which norms would you recommend abandoning? Would you change the way these norms are created and who gets to decide?
- Which definition of "civility" resonates with you more—formal politeness or citizenship? Why? If you define civility to be about good citizenship, how would that change your idea of what constitutes "civil" behavior?
- When you read about college students today being closed-minded, does that resonate with your experience? How does it compare to how you see yourself? If you were to write an opinion piece about your generation of students, what would you want to say? What concerns

facing today's college students would you like the press to pay more attention to?

Writing Exercises for Chapter 3

- This year, voters in the state of West Dakota will vote on a ballot initiative to legalize cannabis. A high school senior at Springfield High (in West Dakota's capital city) displayed a banner that reads "Bong Hits R *STILL* 4 Jesus" at an after-school event about voting and civic engagement. The principal asked you whether the student could be punished. Apply what you know about students' speech rights *and* explain the arguments for and against punishing the student even if a court would permit the principal to do so.
- You are a member of your college president's cabinet. Draft an institutional policy about when the president should issue public statements about speech on campus, including protected and unprotected speech.
- You learned that hateful speech in public spaces—such as carrying a sign that denigrates a group—is constitutionally protected. Imagine you are founding a private university. Unlike a public university, your school may limit some hateful speech. What should they do? If you are inclined to protect all hateful speech from censorship or punishment, write the best argument against doing so. If you are inclined to censor or punish some hateful speech, write the best argument against your position. Whichever side you argue, make sure you define the speech that will be covered by your policy.

- Select a rule of discourse that you would like to eliminate (e.g., rules against profanity; a class community standard on confidentiality; class policies for or against content warnings). Explain why you oppose the rule and, if possible, propose and defend an alternative.
- Write an op-ed (under 750 words) explaining what you think older generations need to know about college students like you when it comes to free expression, dialogue, and open-mindedness.

4

Listen and Read with a Mindset of Informed Generosity and Grace

UNDER WHAT CIRCUMSTANCES is it better to listen and read with an open mind?

> We can disagree and still love each other unless your disagreement is rooted in my oppression and denial of my humanity and right to exist.
>
> —ROBERT JONES JR.[1]

The practice of inquiry in a diverse community involves an enormous amount of reading and listening. It also requires us to hear—and often analyze—texts and statements from a wide variety of perspectives and people. Though most students

1. The quote is often misattributed to the twentieth-century American writer James Baldwin. "About Son of Baldwin," Son of Baldwin, August 18, 2015, https://www.sonofbaldwin.com/contact/.

will take a college writing course, you're unlikely to take a class specifically focused on listening and reading. But college-level listening and reading—like inquiry, writing, or speaking—are skills worth studying.

Why?

Skillful listening and reading—particularly when it results in dialogue between our ideas and authors' and peers' own perspectives—makes our positions more nuanced, our writing more precise, and our thinking more creative. It makes us better; it's the engine for becoming better scholars and communicators ourselves.

If we focus only on the headlines about speech on college campuses, it's easy to forget that the overwhelming bulk of listening and learning across difference doesn't happen in large lecture halls with an invited speaker. It involves reading challenging texts; engaging in classroom discussion; reading and discussing professors' feedback; and seeking constructive dialogue on the issues that matter to us. Dialogues about tough, lovable questions can be wondrous—especially when we navigate points of disagreement.

Actively seeking dissenting views has made my own work infinitely better. One such experience stands out in my memory. Some years ago I was asked to speak at "The Walking Dead," a symposium on legal issues related to death. The conveners knew I had spoken against proposals to legalize physician-assisted suicide—a stance based on my concern for disabled people and that put me in opposition to many of my fellow civil rights lawyers. I looked forward to presenting what

I knew would be a minority opinion on my panel and worked hard to produce a draft statement that would present my position effectively. In the course of my work, I had two conversations that changed my article for the better.

First, I sought out a meeting with a constitutional law professor whom I deeply respect. Over the years, he has been generous with his time and mentorship, and I see him as a role model in my own never-finished effort to be a good teacher of constitutional law. He hated my position! How could someone who had worked to preserve civil liberties oppose such a basic human right as the right to die, he wanted to know. I didn't, I explained. Well, what was my position? What, indeed? Speaking into a barrage of questions and critiques, I improved my ideas: I articulated the circumstances in which legalizing physician-assisted death would not threaten disabled people and explained how far our country was from those circumstances. He didn't buy that either, but my premise had survived an hour with one of the smartest people I've ever met, and my reasoning and position had become more precise. I spent that evening completely reshaping my outline. What had been simple opposition to a bill that morning had become a coherent alternative by the time I went to bed.

The second conversation happened almost by accident. I mentioned the article in passing to another lawyer I was meeting about an unrelated project. My feeling, going into the conversation, was that my own position was the humane one. After all, I was speaking out for disability rights; my position was that the movement for "death with dignity" devalued and degraded disabled lives, and that the political and legal discourse silenced the very people who were most at risk of being pressured into an end of life "choice" that was no choice at all. It would not be an overstatement to say I felt righteous.

However, it turned out my friend had a personal connection to this issue. The story of his friend's illness and death was painful to hear. It illustrated why many people hold a good-faith belief that patients should be able to get a physician's assistance in dying. I hadn't been unaware of those arguments and interests; in fact, my own legal and policy positions already accounted for many of the material concerns expressed. But in sharing my own views, I hadn't expressed my awareness or empathy—only my conclusions and reasoning. My framing and my unwarranted confidence were, to put it mildly, inadequate to the emotional complexity of the topic.

That day, my friend accorded me a kind of grace and patience that I aspire to offer. Instead of scolding or correcting, he offered a different perspective and a chance to do better. Education is about growth; offering feedback and an opportunity to do better is education. It's what I hope to bring to my classrooms and to the tough conversations in my life.

Almost anything worth writing about is going to matter to real people. And it is possible that "winning," even if one's position ends up helping the most people, could come at a cost to others. Understanding that makes better policy and, I would argue, makes us better people. And when we are engaging in classroom dialogue—unlike in my conversation with a friend—our classmates and professors are working from much more limited information, and still forming conclusions. It's always useful to acknowledge complexity—particularly when our words in a class context are the only information about us our listeners have.

Applying Our Habits of Inquiry to Listening and Reading

Conventional wisdom says that we should be open-minded. Particularly in college, I think open-mindedness is a worthy goal. This is a time when we have more opportunities than ever before (and possibly more than we will again) to explore challenging ideas and engage with a wide variety of people. Most of the time, listening with an open mind can teach us something.

But if we make the principle of open mindedness a rule, we see that there are some circumstances where it doesn't apply.

- You are Charlie Brown. Your friend Lucy offers to hold a football for you to kick. The past 100 times, she has pulled it away at the last second, causing you to fall.
- You are studying for your physics midterm. Your roommate asks you to watch a video that presents her position on whether student athletes should be paid. You two were arguing about this at lunch, but now you are focused on your test.
- For your research, you work with a research librarian to construct a search of scholarly publications. Your uncle recommends you also add some YouTube videos exposing a huge government cover-up of the contrary research.

Closing your mind to these voices isn't a bad thing.

The opposite advice—question everything—also fails if we make it a rule:

- You are walking in a remote area of a national park. You come to a water hole and see fresh tracks that look like

your cat's paws, but 5" wide. Your friend tells you there must be a mountain lion nearby, and that you both need to back away and return to your canoe.
- You have pain in your chest and left arm. A quick Google search tells you to seek medical attention immediately.

In either circumstance, acting quickly is the right call. Of course, most conversations do not fall at these extremes. And some conversations that might make us angry or uncomfortable still have worth. Becoming proficient in college and civic dialogue requires considering which hard conversations will be worth engaging in.

A student shared an experience that to me exemplifies listening generously—and bravely. Alicia went on a trip to Israel and Palestine organized by an organization that provides groups of students with multiple perspectives on that region. She explained to me that she was willing to go and learn and that because of her upbringing as a Palestinian, she knew she would need to *unlearn* some of what she knew due to the dominant narratives to which she's been exposed. "I heard one perspective more than another," she explained. It turns out she was the only Arab and Palestinian in her tour group—a challenging position for a young person discussing and exploring issues with a direct impact on her family.

The decision to join such a trip and immerse oneself in conversations that would prove taxing but important sounds like a model for others to follow. But it is also not simple. In fact, my student explained that she continues to process the conversations, changing her mind repeatedly, and doubting she would recommend the experience without some drastic changes. My student emphasized how she had a personal stake in all of the conversations and experiences undertaken; she says that these types of conversations demand more consideration of their difficulties and inherent harm. But her presence on the trip—and her decision to share her perspectives both during and after—have the potential to benefit many other people.

Not all of us will take an immersive ten-day trip across the world to listen to multiple perspectives. But college does offer opportunities for dialogue. In my experience, some of the most successful student dialogues take place in contexts where students are committed to listen generously and have a shared mission to create something together.

A student project in one of my classes exemplifies great dialogue in an academic setting. In my course called "Law and the Political System," I tasked student groups to examine a challenging issue from multiple perspectives, then write the best arguments for both sides of their issues and give presentations about how lawmakers can make policy in these areas, acknowledging the values, concerns, and beliefs that animate people on all sides of the issue.

One group explored the pros and cons of repealing the Second Amendment (the provision of our constitution that protects the right to bear arms). The group included one student who strongly supported the proposition, one who strongly opposed it, and two who were closer to the middle. In approaching their topic, they first explored what experience they all had with firearms. All had some experience, including one student who is a military veteran. Then, they collaboratively explored why someone would want to repeal the Second Amendment and why *someone* would want to preserve it. By collaboratively generating the best arguments for and against, they were able to see the strengths of arguments they did not hold. I recommend both these techniques—inventorying the personal experience and knowledge with a topic and collaboratively considering arguments for and against—in dialogues across difference.

Two features of this particular project are worth considering as you explore your interest in listening generously. First, this topic—though profoundly polarizing in political discourse—is somewhat easier to discuss in a class context than matters pertaining to individuals' identities. As a student in the group explained to me, "it's important but it's not an identity. It's not immutable. Discussing a topic like this is good because it's not immutable." I am not suggesting that students avoid ever trying to discuss matters that touch people much more personally. But as you are building your dialogue skills, it is worth trying topics where you are certain you and your peers can be in conversation without a feeling of personal vulnerability. It is also worthwhile, when in conversation, to consider whether members—including you—will have a personal connection to an issue that warrants care.

Second, this exercise was successful because the students had a shared mission—creating memos and a presentation reflecting their best arguments and advice. As my student explained, "people are afraid to talk in college when it's just the Wild West. When you open the topic up too widely, bad guys will jump all over it." He explained that speaking in small groups and having a shared mission both enable students to hold a productive and rewarding conversation.[2]

2. Caleb Bates video conference interview with Lara Schwartz, January 10, 2023.

The practice of college inquiry demands that we develop principled and balanced approaches to listening and reading. I recommend applying a rebuttable presumption of good faith to people and texts; listening with informed generosity; and taking a restorative, not punitive, response to good-faith mistakes.

A (Rebuttable) Presumption of Good Faith

A presumption is something we take to be true. Presumptions can be "rebuttable," meaning that learning additional facts can overcome our initial judgment. In law, examples of rebuttable presumptions include:

- A person who has been missing for more than seven years is presumed dead.
- A defendant in a criminal trial is presumed innocent.

Both presumptions are rebuttable. If the missing person suddenly appears in a restaurant the law recognizes that she is indeed alive. The prosecution may overcome the presumption of innocence by presenting evidence that persuades a jury beyond a reasonable doubt.

Some presumptions are irrebuttable, or conclusive. A four-year-old child is legally incompetent to consent to a contract. No amount of evidence of the child's extraordinary intelligence or maturity will make a contract with that child enforceable. The child's legal status is not only the result of provable facts (such as their physical and cognitive development); it is based on a policy judgment that children cannot be held responsible for their actions in the same way as adults.

Good Faith

What does it mean to accord a rebuttable presumption of good faith to colleagues and texts? It means assuming people are trying to approach conversations with integrity and decency, and not to troll you. This is the opposite of listening defensively or listening to rebut. In practice, adopting this presumption means showing patience and understanding that as they learn new material, people will make mistakes and be open to feedback.

For example, your professor assigns a text that includes off-putting language, such as a Supreme Court decision that uses antiquated terms for disabled people or a novel with dialogue that includes racial slurs. Applying a presumption of good faith, we would conclude the professor assigned the text to explore its legal significance or artistic merit, not to degrade anyone. There would still be room to critique that decision—in fact, I would encourage the professor to hear criticism with generosity. Listening generously does not require the student to agree that the reading was well chosen, nor require the professor to change the readings. But if they take one another at their word, they can learn something.

When we presume people are engaging in good faith—and not attempting to troll or cause harm—we can listen with generosity, believing that there is something we can learn from the experience. As I'll explore later, it is possible to rebut the presumption of good faith. Furthermore, practicing this presumption can be burdensome—and unequally so. But as a starting point, it enables us to listen openly, and gives all of us space to speak, knowing our good-faith efforts will be received as such.

Why Accord Grace?

First, mistakes are a part of life in a learning community. Students' status as learners means that they are in the process of adapting to higher academic standards, new disciplinary conventions, and new communities. Trying something difficult almost always means doing it imperfectly. When we accord a rebuttable presumption that people are trying in good faith, we can also assume mistakes and even offenses are not malicious. If we recognize that this learning process benefits all parties—not just the person who has made the mistake, but people who will interact with them in the future, we can see that this learning process is worthwhile, even if it is challenging.

Second, we accord forgiveness so we can receive it. In one class discussion, you might show patience with fellow students who do not understand rural life. In the next, they might show patience with your limited experience with public transit. Students cannot arrive at college with a fully developed perspective on every experience, but you can commit to learn, and ask the same of others.

What Is Informed Generosity, and Why Is Presuming Good Faith an Act of Generosity?

I have often heard (and shared) the advice to listen to understand, not to rebut. Listening to understand means applying cognitive skills to the task of comprehension rather than combat. This is sometimes very easy—for example, when seeking technical support for a computer. When we make that call, we know the other person is trying to help, and we're unlikely to have a personal or moral objection to their troubleshooting method. Listening patiently maximizes our capacity to learn from what we are hearing or reading.

Sometimes this kind of listening is harder, such as when we're getting feedback on our writing or the things we say. In my experience, the more I know about a topic, and the more invested I am in a position or my work product, the harder it is to listen to understand. When we feel invested in our ideas or our work, it's not unreasonable to want to defend them. In my experience, that is when listening also has the potential to provide the greatest reward. We can learn a great deal from people who see our work with fresh eyes.

In seeking to turn "listen to understand" into a workable principle for college dialogue, I chose "informed generosity" after considering some alternatives. As someone who enjoys opening my home to guests and (over)feeding them, I love the word "hospitality." But I also felt it implied that the person providing hospitality owns the space. I wouldn't describe myself as hospitable in a shared space like a public park, for example. And since I do not "own" my classes even if I have a lot of power there, hospitality doesn't describe what I or my students are doing when we listen. Generosity, by contrast, is mutual.

Listening generously also expresses two points that I believe are important: first, that our listening has value. Offering a platform is not a value-neutral exercise. And second, presuming good faith, and listening accordingly, is not without its costs. After all, when someone gives us something that cost them nothing and that they didn't value, that is not generosity.

It is only when our actions come at a cost that we can be considered generous.

Our generosity isn't limitless or unprincipled. Practicing informed generosity means applying our principles of inquiry: including relevance, information literacy, and disciplinary standards—when we listen. This enables us to focus on the texts that can help us learn what we need to know; filter out bad-faith or dubiously credible materials; and pursue conversations with purpose.

Informed generosity also means determining whether some conversations are not worth having at all. That could mean avoiding a late-night argument about politics so we can rest before an exam, choosing not to engage with someone who has treated us badly before, or putting off a discussion we're not ready to have—whether because we haven't yet studied the topic deeply enough or because we're still processing grief or anger about it.

Listen Generously to People Who Are Setting Limits in Good Faith

College is a place for expansive inquiry. In general, a default assumption that questions are good, that subject matter is fair game for discussion, and that voices should be heard has proven beneficial. It allows research to thrive, new academic disciplines to evolve and flourish, and new voices to join campus communities.

However, the fact that open-mindedness has generally benefited higher education does not create a duty of every student to be open to hearing every argument. Each of us has the autonomy to set limits—a freedom closely connected to our First Amendment freedoms of expression and association, and to our academic freedom to pursue the subjects of our choice. Listening generously should include treating people's assertion of boundaries with the same generosity we show their expression. This is particularly true because the burdens and challenges of our system of free inquiry are unevenly distributed.

For example: in the coming years, constitutional law students will discuss the scope and ramifications of recent Supreme Court decisions—including a 2022 decision in which the Court overruled the 1973 case of *Roe v. Wade* and ruled that there is no federal constitutional right to abortion. For some students, these conversations will be more than theoretical. They will involve the loss of tangible rights and the question of whether they will lose additional legal rights they currently have (such as the right to marry). These conversations will carry unequal burdens.

In fact, when it comes to law and policy, almost every conversation worth having will affect someone. Take gas prices, which might sound like a neutral subject. High fuel costs will disproportionately affect people with less disposable income, rural people who must travel long distances in their day-to-day life, and those who rely on trucks or heavy machinery for their livelihood (such as farmers and contractors). Almost all politics implicate identity in some way—the question is whose identity, and how.

I will not refrain from holding conversations about hotly contested issues. But I encourage students to practice generosity when their peers—or others—set boundaries for conversation, particularly outside of class. I also encourage everyone to communicate compassionately and be open to feedback about the impact their speech has on others.

I have heard some otherwise well-intentioned people say that students who don't want to engage in tough conversations don't belong in college. But because many contentious conversations affect students unequally, I strongly disagree. Transforming open inquiry from a goal to a rule means treating students who have more at stake in a conversation as if they are somehow less successful at inquiry—when in fact it might cost them more. Listening generously to others' good-faith statements about their boundaries doesn't shut down inquiry; it offers us an opportunity to better understand how important issues affect people, which itself can be a valuable learning experience.

The Mechanics of Listening and Reading Generously

When listening to rebut, our mind asks, "What is missing?" "What did they get wrong?" "What limitations or contradictions do I hear?" Questions like these can be a useful component of constructive criticism. When you critique a peer's draft paper (or edit your own draft), reading with these questions in mind can be helpful.

In a dialogue, particularly in class discussions or when reading a challenging text, I recommend pivoting to the question "What (more) would I need to know in order to understand this perspective fully?" Instead of listening to rebut, allow yourself to be in a state of wonder, and express what you are wondering.

Follow-up questions from generous listeners:

- What would you say is the most important part of your idea?
- Can you help me understand the problem you're solving?
- Can you tell me more about how this would work in practice?
- Are there any limitations you can see to what you're proposing?

Listening Generously to Critics

Anyone who asks for the benefit of the doubt when speaking and writing should also extend it to critics. This is particularly true for people in positions of power and authority (including faculty and employers). Listening with generosity to criticism means according the critic a presumption that they are expressing concern in good faith.

Assuming our critics are acting in good faith means taking them at face value when they tell us we've been hurtful, that we've employed antiquated language, or that our position reflects a stereotype or trope. Remember: speech that falls short of harassment can still be unkind, hurtful, inaccurate, or laden with historical baggage. Our speech and actions can have impacts we never intended. So in college courses, we strive for something better than legally protected speech. We aspire to accuracy, insight, and respect. Feedback that helps us meet those standards is beneficial. That's why I try to show gratitude for feedback.

Moving from a position of defensiveness to gratitude isn't easy, and it doesn't happen overnight. In my experience, people need to feel fully accepted and respected in order to abandon defensiveness. The more we build community and trust, the better able we are to accept feedback gratefully.

When a learning community takes a restorative approach to dialogue—offering opportunities to learn rather than seeking punishment—there is little risk in assuming our critics are acting in good faith. On the other hand, when we take a punitive approach to speech transgressions—seeking steep consequences such as dismissal from a job or expulsion from a school—it is not surprising when speakers mount legalistic defenses to good-faith criticisms.

Intent Is Not Equal to Impact

A legalistic approach will often focus on the speaker's intent rather than the impact of speech. For example, although burning a cross is an expression with a historic connection to terroristic violence, it is not legally a "true threat" absent a showing of intent. Nonetheless, if someone burned a cross without such intent—for example, while filming a movie about American history—a bystander who happened upon the scene could still be terrified.

Expression can have an impact regardless of intent. Oliver Wendell Holmes observed that "even a dog distinguishes between being stumbled over and being kicked." This quotation captures why intent has legal significance. But being stumbled over, much like being kicked, can hurt. There is a difference between a legal ruling that speech is protected and a conclusion that it has no impact. Listening generously to critics means being open to hearing we have had an impact even when we intended no harm.

When someone tells you how they feel, apply a (rebuttable) presumption that they are to be believed. Each of us is the #1 expert on ourselves, after all. Remember that the person's stated feeling can be genuine even if it doesn't reflect what you intended them to feel. Similarly, you can expect the courtesy of belief from others, too. We all benefit from hearing how our actions affect those around us.

The idea that we can be unintentionally hurtful—or unintentionally racist—can be uncomfortable to accept. In the legal arena, claims of unintentional racism don't fare very well.[3] But when we listen generously to feedback and criticism, we can be open to the idea that two things are true at once: that we did not intend to express bigotry or hostility, but our listeners' experiences are real.

Our personal experiences, perspectives, and identities can all contribute to the gap between intent and perception. An example from my own experience demonstrates this. I am a woman and use the prefix "Ms." My son has a different last name than I do. For most of his childhood, doctors' office staff referred to me as "Mrs. (son's last name)" in spite of my repeated corrections. Even though no one intended to hurt my

3. See *Washington v. Davis*, 426 U.S. 229 (1976).

feelings, their assumption bothered me. It's a mistake that not only burdens women more than men but is also a remnant of a system in which women historically did not have independent legal status and autonomy in marriage. Since I became a mother, there have been hundreds of times when people have applied inaccurate and dated assumptions about me that a father would not face. "Mrs. (Not My Last Name)" symbolizes those experiences for me.

When we consider only intent and ignore impact, the office staff's frequent errors cannot be considered unkind. But if we consider the speech in the context of my own experiences with discrimination and stereotyping and in the context of women's experiences beyond that doctor's office, we can understand much more.

On the other hand, when people mispronounce my first name (which happens almost daily), I don't mind at all. The difference between two possible pronunciations of "Lara" has no baggage for me. This is not to say that people are wrong when they express concern about their name being mispronounced. It can be a sign of disrespect—especially in relation to culture, ethnicity, and race. The fact that I don't personally have any hard feelings about people mispronouncing my first name tells you something about my identity—I do not have a name that many Americans consider foreign. These two examples of unintentional mistakes show how circumstances beyond the conversation—including history and identity—can affect whether a thoughtless mistake inflicts hurt.

These examples also serve as a reminder that when we are in dialogue with someone, we meet each other not as blank slates but as the sum total of our prior experiences. By the time I go to my son's doctor's office, I have been called "Mrs. (Not My Last Name)" or "(Not my prefix) Schwartz" many times. By the time a new classmate meets you, she might have corrected the pronunciation of her first name hundreds of times—a minor burden in each instance, but a greater one in the aggregate, and a reminder that in many spaces, she is considered "foreign."

Ask Yourself: What Else Could Be True?

The distinction between intent and impact is just one example of the ways that different parties to a dialogue often have distinct and even contradictory experiences. When faced with a reaction to your speech that you feel contradicts the *truth* of your intentions or words—ask yourself, "What else could be true?"

Your truth: you made a good-faith effort to be kind and considerate. *What else could be true*: the subject matter is more personal to others in the room; the word choice has significance in historical context that was clear to people who have been affected by it.

Does That Mean Everybody Gets to Be Offended about Everything?

Some critics of inclusive dialogue efforts claim the real problem is that everybody is too offended all the time,[4] and that we'd all be better off if people were more resilient. But if we look at college as a training ground for civic life, and college

4. About two-thirds of US adults (65 percent) say that "people being too easily offended" is a major problem in the country today. J. Baxter Oliphant, "For Many Americans, Views of Offensive Speech Aren't Necessarily Clear Cut," Pew Research

discourse as a skill that prepares us for civic dialogue, we see it is worthwhile to listen generously to those who give us feedback about how our speech affects them.

Although in the "real world" disrespectful speech is protected from government punishment, private and individual actors are free to assert their own consequences. People who offend customers will not have customers for very long. Managers whose team members dislike them won't retain staff. Politicians who alienate voters may not win reelection. At the ballot box, we are not obligated to vote based upon an objective, reasonable, or majoritarian interpretation of whether the candidate is racist, sexist, mendacious, or trustworthy. We get to decide for ourselves based on how we perceive the candidate.

When we consider that alienating people has consequences—and that communicating in a way that feels respectful to them has advantages—we can experience feedback as a part of our education, not as a limitation on our freedom. This is possible when we take a restorative approach to communication because we are not offering a critique as part of a process of proving that a person has done wrong; we are offering the possibility that the person can do better.

Demonstrate Empathy in Dialogue

We do not have to agree with our peers' positions to have empathy with their struggles. In a legalistic or punitive model of evaluating communication, participants are weighing whether, on measure, a person is at fault for their distress. In a restorative

Center, December 14, 2021, https://www.pewresearch.org/fact-tank/2021/12/14/for-many-americans-views-of-offensive-speech-arent-necessarily-clear-cut/.

and educational mindset, we are open to the idea that multiple things can be true at once: our peer used an antiquated and inappropriate term, *and* she is embarrassed to have been corrected in front of everyone. My student earned a low grade for a paper with significant errors, *and* he is disappointed about the impact on his GPA. Showing care for someone else's humanity does not mean conceding a point to them; empathy is not a betrayal of principle.

How to Practice Productive Critique in a Restorative Communication Context

In college dialogue—where students and faculty engage in good-faith efforts to learn challenging material and build communication skills—feedback (even criticism) is part of the educational process. When possible, align criticisms with objective standards (much like your own classroom contributions). This gives the speaker or writer an opportunity to understand you and enables you both to develop a shared vocabulary for understanding the problem. Although criticism can be constructive, for some, the word "criticism" carries a negative connotation. Another term for constructive criticism that doesn't have the same baggage is "critique." Whichever term you choose, utilizing an explicit objective standard helps keep your feedback useful.

> *Subjective/standardless criticism*: "What you said was problematic."
>
> *Criticism that incorporates an objective standard* (also known as critique): "You made an unsupported generalization about people who live in rural areas."

If you receive criticism that you don't understand (including subjective criticism), you can ask for more information. For example: "You said my presentation was 'weak'. Could you explain how it fell short of the assignment requirements, or what you believe it did not accomplish?"

A note on peer critique: Questions are an excellent form of critique. Rather than "correcting" a peer's paper, engage in dialogue with a writer by asking questions that their text brings up for you.

Where Appropriate, Call In

When our goal is to help the speaker or writer do better, it's helpful to offer feedback that offers them space to do so. Justice advocate and professor Loretta Ross describes this practice as "calling in."[5] While calling *out* generally involves publicly drawing attention to transgressions, sometimes with the intention to shame or punish, "calling in is speaking up without tearing down. A call-in can happen publicly or privately, but its key feature is that it's done with love. Instead of shaming someone who's made a mistake, we can patiently ask questions to explore what was going on and why the speaker chose their harmful language."[6]

Calling in—offering feedback that is educational and restorative—is an appropriate response to good-faith errors and

5. Loretta Ross, "Speaking Up Without Tearing Down," *Learning for Justice* 61 (Spring 2019), https://www.learningforjustice.org/magazine/spring-2019/speaking-up-without-tearing-down.

6. Ross, "Speaking Up Without Tearing Down."

in the context of constructive dialogue and education. Calling in looks a lot like the practice of inquiry and loving questions that we have already explored. It includes the practice of pausing for reflection and further learning. Calling in can also involve the entire classroom in the education process, rather than focusing on punishing a particular person for their conduct.

Unlike calling out—which often consists of naming the harm and who is responsible for it—calling in can involve asking questions designed to spur further reflection. For example, I might ask a student if they are aware of other perspectives on the issue at hand or whether they want to clarify their intent. In my own classroom I call in by facilitating a discussion of what we would need to know to evaluate or critique the claim being made—rather than simply stating that the claim is wrong.[7]

Sometimes, I call out—articulate a judgment about specific behavior and the harm it causes. This can be appropriate when someone is engaging in malicious or harassing behavior or when I am critiquing a powerful figure or institution. But because I hold more power in classroom conversations than my students, and I hope to hold productive three-month conversations in an atmosphere of trust, I strongly prefer calling in.

How students choose to engage with one another—calling in or calling out—is your choice. Calling in takes more work than calling out, and like other forms of generous dialogue, can impose an unequal burden on some students. On the

7. For examples of useful probing questions, see Gene Thompson-Grove, "The School Reform Initiative Pocket Guide to Probing Questions," School Reform Initiative, last updated March 30, 2017, https://www.schoolreforminitiative.org/download/pocket-guide-to-probing-questions/.

other hand, calling in opens the possibility for both change and accountability, which makes it a worthwhile investment for members of a close learning community.

Where Would You Draw the Line? Limitations on Listening with Generosity

Listening generously doesn't mean listening limitlessly. If it did, we'd never make a deadline to turn in a research paper. There are many reasons to stop listening—including when a speaker or text overcomes your presumption of good faith. This could happen when you conclude a source isn't credible or when someone disrespects your good-faith request for boundaries or respect. When you write a research paper, there is no obligation to check whether conspiracy websites have finally said something credible. There will be times when interactions with people overcome the presumption of good faith, and we find we are dealing with a troll, someone who wants to cause chaos, or someone who doesn't share our commitment to learning. Stepping away from those conversations is often described as an act of self-care. It also happens to be an act of expressive freedom.

But this framework of listening and reading—in which students are asked to have an open mind unless and until there is a reason to close it—is not without its burdens and drawbacks. I describe this approach as "generosity" because it offers the speakers something of value, and because it comes with costs that are unevenly distributed. In many college classrooms, a small number of people of color can be expected to carry the burden of sharing their perspective for the majority. In many workplaces, including in academia, the small number of underrepresented minorities—such as faculty and staff of color—are asked to perform extra service in the form of mentoring and representing their perspectives on committees.[8]

Listening Is Valuable

You've probably heard the expression that time is money. We rent out our time to employers in exchange for wages. We use the language of value to describe how we use time—we *spend* it. Students pay tuition based on credit hours—and the college in turn provides instructional time, including the class. As a student, you will decide how much of your time to spend studying for your courses, earning money to pay tuition and expenses, enjoying your life (hopefully), or engaging in conversations about tough issues.

When a student offers a comment in class, they are choosing to spend not only their own instructional time, but classmates' as well. Time is a limited resource, and everyone is best off if students and faculty treat it as such. If members of your class are taking their responsibilities as speakers seriously—following disciplinary norms (or thoughtfully challenging them), preparing for class, and communicating to be understood, listening generously is worth it.

8. JoAnn Trejo, "The Burden of Service for Faculty of Color to Achieve Diversity and Inclusion: The Minority Tax," American Society for Cell Biology, December 1, 2020, https://www.ncbi.nlm.nih.gov/pmc/articles/PMC7851863/.

If, on the other hand, students are trolling one another, monopolizing discussion, or failing to prepare, class discussion can be boring or downright hard. Students might find they are out of generosity by mid-semester, particularly if there are classroom actors in constant conflict with one another. If this is happening in your class, take advantage of office hours or mid-semester feedback surveys to let your instructor know. It helps faculty to hear a student perspective.

Controversies about invited speakers often center on the claim that schools are offering the hateful speaker a valuable platform. You now know that the First Amendment prohibits public schools from denying that platform. But when private colleges voluntarily extend space for a speaker to be heard, the claim that they are being given something of value is worth considering.

Students are not required to attend these events. Therefore, the decision whether to lend one's ears by attending—even if only to challenge a speaker—is different from a public school's nondecision to host a speaker, or an administrator's nondecision to comply with a school's voluntary policy.

Some students decide to protest speakers and/or protest their school's decision to grant speakers a platform. Protest is a protected form of expression. School protest policies often note that protest must not deny other people access to events—whether by blocking their path, preventing the event from taking place, or drowning out the speaker. Counter-speech that contradicts a guest speaker is protected, so long as it doesn't actually prevent the speaker from speaking or being heard.

Listening Generously Comes with a Cost

There are (at least) two ways of thinking about expressive freedom. One is that this freedom yields great results (the Triumphalist model). Another is that it's the least bad way of making space for great results (the Realist model).[9] There is some evidence that free speech, as constitutional law professor Garrett Epps has written, isn't free.[10] If speech had no impact, it would not be worth protecting. Examples of protected speech that comes with a cost include misinformation. As I write this, misinformation about elections has caused many people to distrust our democracy and has even led some to commit violence. Dehumanizing statements are also protected in the public square but come with a cost. Propaganda campaigns mischaracterizing groups of people as threats or less than human have been precursors to genocide.[11]

If we look at what the speech marketplace is offering, there is indeed a lot of junk. In a classroom, though, many of the worst products we might find online (conspiracy theories, genocidal propaganda) are largely absent. Still, even unintentionally insulting speech can do harm by making the classroom environment less welcoming to the person targeted.

9. "Free Speech Isn't Free: A Conversation with Garrett Epps," American University Project on Civil Discourse, YouTube, October 17, 2008, https://www.youtube.com/watch?v=Auows9nAxwI&t=29s.

10. Garrett Epps, "Free Speech Isn't Free," *The Atlantic*, February 7, 2014, https://www.theatlantic.com/politics/archive/2014/02/free-speech-isnt-free/283672/.

11. See "Dangerous Speech: A Practical Guide," The Dangerous Speech Project, April 19, 2021, https://dangerousspeech.org/guide/.

The Unequal Burdens of Generosity and Grace

When we accord a presumption of good faith and offer grace in response to mistakes, we make space for everyone to learn. This is particularly important in college classrooms, where peer groups of nonexperts are exposed to new academic disciplines, concepts, and standards. Although these practices are beneficial to learning communities, they can burden some students more than others.

The burdens of generosity are unequal because our shared knowledge and points of ignorance are unequal. College students usually have very similar levels of knowledge about course subject matter, but their knowledge of each other's cultures, religions, perspectives, traditions, and experiences varies widely. For example, even members of minority religions in the United States are bound to know when Christmas is. Because it's a federal holiday, government offices and public schools are closed. Students don't have classes or exams on Christmas. Unless you work in public safety, health, the military, or hospitality, you are likely to get Christmas day off. Your friends are very unlikely to schedule a study session, ask for your help moving apartments, or ask you to explain why you're not available for either of these things on December 25. If you celebrate Christmas, the chance you'll have to explain it or make any effort to adjust your college work to accommodate it are vanishingly small in the United States. By contrast, students who observe Jewish, Muslim, Hindu, or other non-Christian holidays will have to seek accommodations for time off and will often have to explain themselves to their professors and peers.

This is just one example of the ways our identity or background affects how much explaining, correcting, and educating each of us might have to do in a diverse learning community. College and civic dialogue also involve an unequal distribution of knowledge, ignorance, and the labor required to explain—particularly around matters of religion, language, culture, and history. In any college classroom, there will be some shared knowledge that most participants have, and differences that can make students feel like outliers. Shared knowledge will vary depending upon what country, region, or state you are in.

In some ways, college classrooms reflect larger societal defaults: students at most colleges are more likely to be heterosexual, white, and Christian than not. But in other ways, college classes are unrepresentative. Students at four-year colleges are far less likely than the general population to come from poor households;[12] far more likely to come from high-wealth households;[13] and more likely to have parents who went to college too.[14] As a result, some people (particularly first-generation college students and people from low-income

12. Dalia Faheid, "Fewer Students in Class of 2020 Went Straight to College," EducationWeek, April 6, 2021, https://www.edweek.org/teaching-learning/fewer-students-in-class-of-2020-went-straight-to-college/2021/04.

13. Gregor Aisch, Larry Buchanan, Amanda Cox, and Kevin Quealy, "Some Colleges Have More Students from the Top 1 Percent Than the Bottom 60. Find Yours," *New York Times*, January 18, 2017, https://www.nytimes.com/interactive/2017/01/18/upshot/some-colleges-have-more-students-from-the-top-1-percent-than-the-bottom-60.html.

14. Grace Bird, "The Impact of Parents' Education Levels," *Inside Higher Ed*, February 8, 2018, https://www.insidehighered.com/news/2018/02/08/students-postsecondary-education-arcs-affected-parents-college-backgrounds-study.

households) might find themselves as outliers. They might also find themselves having to accord grace to their peers who have limited understanding of their experience.

Lessening the Unequal Burdens of Generosity

In a community where members are expected to forgive good-faith mistakes, we can lighten the burden of those mistakes by educating ourselves. This can include taking classes about cultures, traditions, language, religions, and art that are unfamiliar to us; reading widely, including literature and journalism by diverse authors; attending events; and listening generously and with curiosity to the people around us. Each of us should keep pursuing broader understanding, and not burden community members with additional roles as unpaid cultural educators.

Make Space for Other Voices

In the classroom, you can make space by waiting to raise a hand until after a speaker has finished talking (if your hand is up, you are focused on responding before the other person has finished their thought). Making space for other voices means engaging deeply with what you hear and responding or building on other students' points.

If you find yourself with a platform, such as serving on the editorial board of a student newspaper, working on the university lecture board, or working at an internship where you organize panels and speakers, make space for voices who can add something to the conversation. Making space for other voices starts with listening to people who have been working on and are affected by the issues that interest you. This includes people in your broader community who might not be members of the university community.

Engage with Varied Disciplines and Perspectives, and Improve Your Listening Skills

At a time when American politics is extremely polarized, many writers caution against limiting oneself to "bubbles," small slivers of the broad spectrum of ideas and perspectives that make up our country and world. Some claim that colleges have insufficient intellectual diversity, which they define in partisan (Republican or Democrat) or ideological (liberal or conservative) terms.[15] Although I agree that exposure to varying perspectives is essential to education and civic life, simply reading materials by individuals who identify with one partisan camp or the other does not provide us the tools of inquiry that other types of listening can provide.

For example, if we make the effort to read the self-described liberal and conservative columnists on the *Washington Post* and *New York Times* opinion pages, we will mostly just get the perspective of professional writers in large cities who are selected for their political views, not necessarily for their expertise. As someone who works in higher education, I'm attuned

15. Steven F. Hayward, "Lack of Campus Intellectual Diversity: Primarily a Problem of Ideological Hostility—or Partly a Methodological Problem?" Bipartisan Policy Center, December 18, 2019, https://bipartisanpolicy.org/blog/lack-of-campus-intellectual-diversity-primarily-a-problem-of-ideological-hostility-or-partly-a-methodological-problem/.

to what these commentators miss about life on campuses.[16] I often wonder what they are missing when they comment on topics with which I'm less familiar.

Familiarizing ourselves with the language and methods of multiple academic disciplines can give us the tools to recognize good arguments and know when we need to inquire further. When we study a new discipline, we learn to listen like those who practice that discipline, and those varied types of listening approaches, taken together, enable us to critically examine all kinds of texts and claims, and to curate and develop our own.

To understand what I mean, let's go back to (fictitious) Springfield State University, where community members are engaged in dialogue about the campus's history. Let's say we are at a faculty meeting at SSU, and the conversation turns to students wearing and displaying images of the Confederate flag. If you are listening like a lawyer, you are thinking about whether SSU is public or private and whether the students are directing their expression at particular people in a harassing manner. If you are a historian, you might listen for details about which flag is being displayed and whether it is displayed in connection with explanations or other symbols. If you are listening as a psychologist, you might be attuned to information about students' reactions and well-being.

Studying broadly, across disciplines, is a method of training yourself as a skilled listener. The good news about this is that it's fun. When you learn to listen like a lawyer, historian,

16. There are exceptions. *New York Times* opinion columnist Tressie McMillan Cottom is a sociologist and professor whose scholarship focuses on higher education. But most high-profile columnists writing about college are not experts.

psychologist, or sociologist does, you find your brain seeing important details that you'd overlooked before. It's like if you take up birdwatching, you suddenly notice how many species there are to see in your own neighborhood. Or if you study architecture, you start to notice the details in buildings all around you. In college, you will have opportunities to learn across disciplines not only through your course work, but by listening to teammates, friends, and other peers who are pursuing different courses of study.

Listen for Who Is Being Centered

Writing and research can be expressions of the author's or publication's priorities and concerns. Arguments and claims can be framed to put a particular person, group, or priority at the center. Listening for who and what is *centered* can improve our scholarship and our efforts to be inclusive.

Take, for example, an article reporting that millennials are killing the golf industry.[17] The point of concern in this article includes companies that make golf equipment, investors in golf courses, and the people who work there, among others. But what about the other parties playing a role? If we notice that they have not been centered, we will broaden our inquiry to include these millennials, asking why they are so hell bent on killing golf.

What would we need to know to fully understand why millennials don't play as much golf as their forebears? We could

17. Mallory Schlossberg, "Millennials Are Killing the Golf Industry," *Business Insider*, July 1, 2016, https://www.businessinsider.com/millennials-are-hurting-the-golf-industry-2016-7.

start with their interests and values. If we find that they have concerns about the environmental impact of golf courses, our inquiry will broaden beyond one industry to the broader economy and to people not considered in the original article. This invites challenging questions that the original frame does not (such as whether we actually want to save the golf industry or just help people transition to other work).

Our inquiry could also lead us to the question whether millennials actually like golf but can't afford to play it. Following this line of inquiry, we would find a whole ecosystem of policies and circumstances that led millennials to lack the means to play. What expenses do younger people have compared to previous generations? What policies are behind these generational disparities?

Now we've widened our inquiry into the broader economy and how it affects vast numbers of people, including, in fact, millennials who work in the industry. Thus, we haven't left out the golf industry, but we have learned about a much broader array of concerns.

Looking at headlines is one way to see who is being centered. Considering the way questions are framed is another. Take these two questions:

> Are you concerned that many people today are afraid to speak their minds for fear of giving offense?
>
> Are you concerned that some people are more often the target of hateful rhetoric than others?

The first question centers the speakers and the second centers the people affected by their speech. This example illustrates that the framing can appear to be neutral—"speakers" and "spoken of" sound like categories that could include any of us depending upon context. However, when our topic is hateful rhetoric, the category of speaker and spoken of is more likely to track categories of people who are frequently the targets of hateful speech. People of color, people from a minority religion, immigrants, disabled people, and LGBTQ people are more likely to be targeted by hateful speech.[18] The question's wording reflects who is centered, which not only narrows the range of inquiry (as in our golf industry example), but also obscures equity concerns.

That is why listening for who is being centered is useful both in your efforts to be a good scholar and in your efforts to be kind and equitable. When we listen for who is being centered, we understand how the speaker or writer is trying to deploy their data, whom they're prioritizing, and whose sympathies they want. We can then consider how this ecosystem of data would look if we centered someone else. Listening for who is being centered also invites us to inquire who has been left out.

When considering who is being centered, ask: Who is the author or speaker most concerned about? Who else is involved? What (and who) is being left out of this discussion?

Listen like a Dialogue Facilitator

We explored the difference between middle ground (a compromise between two positions) and common ground (shared priorities, values, and common language regardless of position).

18. "What Is Hate Speech?" United Nations, https://www.un.org/en/hate-speech/understanding-hate-speech/what-is-hate-speech (accessed June 16, 2023).

Dialogue facilitators employ their listening tools to find and draw attention to common ground. Listening like a facilitator means listening with purpose, seeking ways to help the productive threads of conversation flourish, and noticing the variety of priorities, concerns, emotions, skills, and facts that participants are bringing to the room.

Students whom I train as facilitators report that one of the hardest and most rewarding aspects of the job is surrendering their default position as a combatant and assuming a new role as an advocate for inquiry, collaboration, and understanding. Regardless of whether your school has dialogue facilitator training, you can practice listening like a facilitator by trying these skills:

- Make an effort to understand the points you are hearing and the interests behind them.
- Listen for different types of knowledge being deployed within the same conversation, and respect them all.
- Seek objective or disciplinary standards that participants might agree to.
- Acknowledge emotions.
- Be comfortable with high emotion and even conflict (but not personal attacks).
- Acknowledge and point out points for further inquiry and study.
- Model humility.
- Model gratitude for feedback.
- Listen for undefined terms and seek clarification.
- Encourage participants to consider that multiple things can be true at once.

Is This Workable? The Paradox of Tolerance

There is a theory that encapsulates the downside of the generous listening model (and liberalism in general): the Paradox of Tolerance. The philosopher Karl Popper described this paradox—that unlimited tolerance must lead to the disappearance of tolerance.[19] That is because if society tolerates, for example, a despotic or tyrannical movement that is intolerant of opposing views, the intolerant will overcome the tolerant, and there will be no more free society.

There are many ways institutions and governments grapple with this paradox. In some European countries, Nazi symbols such as swastikas, along with holocaust denial, are banned.[20] Such bans would violate the First Amendment if we attempted to enact them in the United States. The First Amendment itself (along with other amendments in the Bill of Rights) presents another answer to the Paradox of Tolerance: it removes censorship from the government's tool kit, forcing society to address problems like hatred and misinformation through other means, but also (hopefully) denying the intolerant the opportunity to use the government to suppress dissent.

In setting limits on the kinds of laws legislatures can enact, our Constitution also attempts to strike a balance between limitless tolerance and the danger of tyranny. As constitutional law professor Louis Michael Seidman has observed, the First Amendment has the effect of limiting speech and

19. Karl Popper, *The Open Society and Its Enemies* (London: Routledge, 2011).

20. Anna Sauerbrey, "How Germany Deals with Neo-Nazis," *New York Times*, August 23, 2017, https://www.nytimes.com/2017/08/23/opinion/germany-neo-nazis-charlottesville.html.

freedom of thought—insofar as it shuts down conversations about whether speech may be limited.[21] He explains: "If the Constitution requires something, then that is the end of the argument, at least in American constitutional culture. Short of constitutional amendment, a constitutional requirement that a thing must be done just means that it must be done. Once the requirement is established, there is nothing left to talk about."

In college classrooms—even in public universities—the First Amendment does not provide an answer to the question of how to define the extent and limits of our own tolerance, under what circumstances we should draw boundaries about what we want to listen to, and when we would wish to distance ourselves from speech—even if we cannot, or would not want to, censor or punish it.

Finding the Line between Disagreement and "Denial of My Humanity"

In my own courses and workshops, when I ask students or faculty how they would define the limitations of their capacity or willingness to listen, they often draw the line with arguments that dehumanize them or threaten them due to who they are. This is hard to dispute. Very few of us are so committed to open mindedness that we would consent to entertain the question whether we have the right to exist.

Yet much like "hate" speech, dehumanizing speech is hard to define. Everyone would agree that a speaker advocating genocide

21. Louis Michael Siedman, "Can Free Speech Be Progressive?" Columbia Law Review 118, no. 7 (2018), https://columbialawreview.org/content/can-free-speech-be-progressive/.

would literally be denying a group's right to exist. It would be harder to find universal agreement about what that means in practice. Does depicting US history in a positive light constitute an implicit argument that indigenous people did not have a right to exist? Who would decide?

In class discussions where we have attempted to distinguish between neutral policy conversations and dehumanizing ones, students have indicated that debating a minimum wage increase is an easy example of a neutral policy discussion. And yet a worker who is food-insecure might experience a debate over the minimum wage increase as being about whether they have a right to survive. Many discussions about important and contested matters are life or death to someone.

Is There an "Extremism" Exception?

Scholars of extremism have attempted to define a line between ordinary disagreement and the extreme ideologies that lead to war and terrorism. One author has described extremism as an ideology that divides society into "us" and "them" and defines violence as the only solution to the "problem" of difference.[22] The language of extremism evokes threat: the other is described as contagion, invasion, usurper. Marchers at the Unite the Right rally chanting "Jews will not replace us" is an example of the extremist language of threat. They were invoking the idea of a zero-sum game between "us" and the other, whose continued presence was a threat to the settled order and the dominant group.

In communities that reject censorship or punishment for protected speech, recognizing extremist ideology and language

22. See J. M. Berger, *Extremism* (Cambridge, MA: The MIT Press, 2018).

is becoming a necessary component of information literacy. Fortunately, there are many resources to support students, faculty, and other community members in recognizing and addressing extremism—the ideology that outgroups are a threat and violence is the answer.[23]

In a system where transgressive speech results in punishment and exclusion, the stakes in defining acceptable or unacceptable speech are very high. When we take a restorative approach to the harms and transgressions that come with open dialogue, precision becomes less important. We can listen generously, including to claims that speech is intolerant or hurtful. Knowing that this is all constructive feedback, and that the "consequence" is that we are better educated about our peers (and free to decide how we use that information), there is no need for defensiveness, and nothing to litigate.

Discussion Questions and Classroom Exercises for Chapter 4

- *Goal setting:* What would you like to learn more about? What topics related to our class would you like to have challenging discussions about?
- *Listening and responsibility:* What are the benefits of listening to understand? Why is it sometimes difficult to listen? What can we do to develop our capacity to listen

23. See Polarization & Extremism Research & Innovation Lab (PERIL), an organization that designs tools and intervention strategies "to prevent hate, bias, and extremist radicalization. PERIL has resources for parents and caregivers, educators, community members, faith and business leaders, and governments," as http://perilresearch.com/ (accessed July 11, 2023).

across difference? What can we do when our conversations become challenging or painful? What responsibilities do we have toward the people who are listening to us?

- Under what circumstances should a classroom community agree to boundaries on what is discussed in class? These fact patterns can help you consider the question. Think broadly about solutions that include both inquiry and respect.
    1. Your political science course includes a veteran of the wars in Iraq and Afghanistan. They say they lost close friends in combat, and that calling recent wars "pointless" is insulting.
    2. You are a peer educator for a first-year experience course. One of your students indicates that they do not feel comfortable attending on the day when your class will discuss intimate partner violence.
- How does your own identity or experience affect your values about being resilient to offense or taking care to avoid offense? In what contexts are you less likely to take offense (for example, among friends)? In what contexts would you expect other speakers to take more care in communicating with you?
- Consider a time when you have wanted to call someone out for their speech and actions in a class (or have done so). What would "calling in" have looked like in that situation? Consider a time you have been called out or called in. What was that like? What did you take away from the conversation? Would you want to build calling in practices into your classroom community agreement or ground rules? What would that look like?

- Schools that recognize their platforms are being used for speech with which the institution does not agree (for example, misinformation or racist speech) sometimes encourage students to attend controversial events and raise their own voices during question and answer. What would we need to know in order to determine whether this is a productive approach?
- What would we need to know to determine whether the triumphalist model or the realist model of free speech more accurately describes the system we have?
- Consider the knowledge you assume your classmates share. For example, references to popular movies or TV shows; local foods or events; religious practices or civic holidays like Thanksgiving (in the United States). Which of your shared experiences would be unfamiliar to someone from another country, state, or region? Are there cultural norms that you assume are shared but that might not be common to everyone (for example, most Americans celebrate Christmas, but many do not)?
- Under what circumstances might tolerating intolerance lead to the triumph of intolerance over a free society? What would we need to know to evaluate Popper's idea (the Paradox)?
- What are some barriers to listening generously? Do you find such barriers on your own campus? What are some steps that your institution could take that would make it easier to listen generously in your community?
- Many campus conduct codes protect peaceful counter-speech and protest that does not prevent a speaker's message from being heard. Under what circumstances

would you approve actions that interfered with a speaker's message?[24]

Writing Exercises for Chapter 4

- *Centering:* Select an article (straight news or opinion). Identify who is being centered. Write an alternative article from the perspective of someone who is not the primary focus.
- *Peer critique:* Trade papers with a peer. Read one another's papers. Do not provide suggested edits. Instead, ask questions (in the margins or with the comment function). Examples of constructive questions for peer critique:
  - What do you mean by __________?
  - How do you define __________?
  - How does this relate to (relevant course text)?
  - Where would you draw the line? Would this idea also apply to __________?
  - What are the arguments against this claim, and how can you address them to strengthen your point?
- *Calling in and calling out*:
  - *Literature/film*: Select a scene from a course reading, a work of literature, or a movie in which two characters

24. Consider Angel Action. When Matthew Shepard, a young gay college student, was murdered, anti-gay protesters appeared at his funeral. Shepard's friend organized people to wear angel costumes with large wings that blocked the protesters from view. Since then, others have used this tactic—which is nonviolent and silent but prevents people from getting their message across.

    are in conflict or in which a character is treating others poorly. Imagine you inhabit this world and could interact with the characters. Is this a time when you would call in or call out, and why? What would your calling in or out look like? Write new dialogue for your new character and those they are engaging with.
    - *Public affairs and current events*: Select a statement by a public official or candidate that you believe is wrong in some way. Imagine you work for a group that works on this issue. Is this a circumstance where you would call in or call out? Write a memo to your organization's staff explaining what you recommend, and why.
- *Campus life*: In a brief, casual conversation after class, a classmate mistook you for someone else who shares some of your characteristics. Is this an occasion to call out, call in, ignore? How might your identity and experience affect your answer?
- Dialogue across difference project: Work in a pair or a group to explore a proposal about which you and your partner/group members disagree (for example: capital punishment should be abolished). Collaboratively explore what you would need to know in order to be fully informed about the issue. Explore evidence-based arguments for and against the proposal. Explore and explain the nature of the positions, values, priorities, and interests motivating proponents and opponents (including yourselves), and the origins and nature of disagreement. Identify common ground among participants. Collaboratively write: the best arguments for the proposal; the best arguments against it; and advice to

others about how to address this issue in light of the good-faith disagreement that exists around it.

- *What else could be true:*
  - *Literature*: Select a scene from a book where two people are in conflict. Write the scene from a new perspective.
  - *Law and freedom of expression*: Consider the case of *Village of Skokie v. National Socialist Party of America*,[25] in which the Illinois Supreme Court ruled that displaying Swastikas in a town populated by many Jews, including Holocaust survivors, was protected expression under the First Amendment. Explain what else is true. In doing so, you can consider the facts from the perspective of the residents, historians, psychologists, teachers, or any other discipline or perspective you choose.

25. *Village of Skokie v. Nat'l Socialist Party of America*, 69 Ill. 2d 605 (1978).

5

Communicate to Be Understood

UNDER WHAT CIRCUMSTANCES is it beneficial to take care about how we communicate?

We practice academic speech in a system of structured liberty. Authorities cannot punish our decisions about the direction our research will take, the positions we express in the public square, or whether we agree with assigned texts or our classmates. Yet standards of evidence, research, and writing apply to our work. In this chapter I will explore what it means to make the paradigm shift from speech rights (what can we say) to speech responsibilities (what should we say) in college and beyond. Communicating to be understood (rather than to dominate, shame, attack, or win) is a practice that centers speech responsibilities—including awareness of our impact on the audience.

Before I came to college teaching from a career as a legislative lawyer, I assumed practicing kindness and care in speech was uncontroversial. In my job I had to speak to, and write for, people and groups ranging from faith communities to US senators to the readers of national and local newspapers. I spoke to congressional staff from every state and to community groups in dozens of cities and towns. Sometimes my work required me to state hard truths about elected officials or candidates—most commonly that they opposed or were seeking to limit civil rights. I took care to craft those critical messages even more carefully than my messages of support for policies and candidates. If your job involves tough conversations, it's wise to communicate with care and precision.

As you now know, speech regulation—particularly punitive responses to transgressive speech—can violate the First Amendment, academic freedom, and the liberal norm of intellectual freedom. However, we go to college to become better at all kinds of things. That includes communicating respectfully with varied and diverse audiences. So it makes sense that professors and, to an extent, college administrations would be making efforts to help students communicate in a way that respects everyone.

However, since I began teaching college full time, I've been exposed to the increasingly urgent message that there is something nefarious about asking students and faculty to communicate with care. Critics of diversity and equity programing are concerned that these efforts are meant to suppress some viewpoints—not promote kindness. And critics of civil discourse are often concerned that calls to open-mindedness are really demands that people tolerate or welcome hateful or exclusionary speech. Many books, articles, and conferences proliferate one of these arguments or the other. I cannot claim to know a perfect balance between kindness and freedom, but I do know that engaged classrooms require both.

A prevailing narrative says that colleges today are getting the balance wrong, and that (some) people can no longer say what they think and that's bad. This doesn't look like college as I know it, nor does it adequately capture what the work of college should be. People playing a preassigned ideological role (liberal, moderate, conservative) and then voicing their opinions without regard to impact sounds more like the TV talk show *The View* than a college classroom. On *The View*, participants have a seat at the table to represent conservatives, liberals, or moderates. But in a classroom, participants have a seat at the table because they are scholars. On the show, the ideological teams are supposed to receive equal time. In a classroom, preparation—not affiliation—drives participation.

Opinion formation and discourse in a college classroom reflect more than political identity; they result from the process we explored in the preceding sections:

1. Inquiry. Students and faculty consider "what would we need to know" to form a position. This can take the form of assigning readings (faculty), researching the topic (individual students or groups), establishing comprehension (during reading time and in class time), and applying, analyzing, critiquing, comparing, and synthesizing texts (in class or in writing).
2. Listening and reading with generosity. Students and faculty read challenging texts and listen to one another, applying a presumption that there is something to be learned from the exercise.

Along with inquiring collaboratively and listening generously, constructive dialogue involves a distinctive form of communication.

3. Communicating to be understood. Discussions are about collaboration, not combat, and participants make good-faith efforts to convey their ideas in a way that will enable engagement, discussion, improvement, and feedback.

If you think this sounds like a lot more work than just saying what you think, you're right. It's also more rewarding. This kind of communication provides an opportunity to test and refine our ideas and positions and challenges us to connect with audiences, which requires developing a broad and deep toolkit of communication skills.

Communicating to be understood is what happens when we shift our mindset:

- *From rights to responsibilities.* Refining our communication, accepting feedback, and being responsive to audience perceptions and needs is a skill worth mastering, not a limitation on freedom.
- *From punitive to restorative responses.* Improving our accuracy and precision requires being open to listeners' concerns, and also requires second (and third, and subsequent) chances to build and use our voices.
- *From debate to inquiry.* Making our best efforts to make our communication accessible, offering ideas that help explore complex subject matter and master concepts being explored in the course, and engaging peers as collaborators, not combatants.

From "Civil" Discourse to Productive (or Purposive) Discourse

People enter college classrooms with differing perspectives and preferences, but with a shared goal connected to the course objectives. This is one reason college courses have the potential to germinate rich, interesting conversations that might not be possible elsewhere. Classes have the potential for productive discourse. Once you have learned to engage deeply and with a purpose, you can apply this approach in other arenas—such as advocating for change in your community.

At first blush, the term "productive" doesn't sound lovable. It might evoke images of a commercial enterprise where we are accountable for producing a certain amount to earn our keep. You might find yourself wanting to remind me that this journey was supposed to be about loving the questions, not meeting a quota of useful communication. To my way of thinking, there is no contradiction here. Often, it's the love of an endeavor—whether trying to understand a new friend's perspective or taking the music lessons we've always wanted—that brings the most energy and productive output. If you'd like, you can also aspire to engage in college discourse that is purposive—serving goals and driven by intention.

Purposive Communication and the College Classroom

To understand the values and habits that make for successful classroom discourse, it helps to consider what class time is for. Many college-level courses (and some high school classes) include a "class participation" grade, but in my experience very few people discuss what goes into that grade. Students who are eager to establish a strong GPA often assume a class participation grade is based on raising one's hand frequently or making sure to comment in every class period. But that kind of participation—though it can demonstrate valuable academic progress—doesn't always mean the person is best prepared or most insightful. It's certainly not the only way to demonstrate what you've learned or contribute to your learning community. By the time you've been in college for a few weeks, you'll see that speaking and contributing are not necessarily the same thing—particularly if you have a classmate who tends to dominate discussion. Your professors see that too.

Early in my college teaching career, I saw first-hand how this narrow vision of "class participation" fell short when I read a masterful final paper by a student who had barely spoken in class. My first thought was that we had all missed out on her insights for three months. My second was that if I wanted my class to be a place where great ideas were shared, thoughtful students spoke up, and all my grading was as fair as possible, I had some work to do.

What I learned has changed the way I solicit and evaluate student participation (which I now call "course engagement").

Now, I take several steps each semester to lay the groundwork for better engagement. I share my hopes and expectations in writing; I hold a class discussion about how we expect to use class time. I ask students to set goals for class time, share them with me, and reflect upon them at semester's end. Even if this doesn't happen in your classes, you can ask your professors about their expectations in office hours, by email, or in class. And what I have learned can help you understand and use classroom time too.

What does meaningful engagement include?

Myth: Asking a question in class makes you look less prepared than you should be.
Fact: A thoughtful question can show that you've reflected on the readings and can help you and the class engage more deeply with the course material.
Action item: When taking notes, make a point of writing down the most interesting or pressing questions the course readings raise for you.

Although raising your hand and speaking aloud aren't the only ways to contribute, this kind of course engagement can be useful for more than just a grade. Testing out your ideas in front of others can help you refine them before including them in a paper. Asking a question helps you and your classmates understand the trickiest aspects of the reading and helps your professor get a read on how well the class understands course material. Speaking in class is good practice for other contexts where you'll need to speak in front of groups (such as at work or in student organizations). Some students come to college adept at speaking in class, while others want to build that skill. The reflection questions at the end of this book will ask you about your goals for speaking up—or, if this is something you are already adept at—for listening and refining your communication.

At the beginning of each semester, I now tell my students that their course engagement grade can include any or all the following:

> Asking or responding to questions; contributing to discussions on the course's online discussion boards; attending office hours; improving your contributions over time; contributing to small group discussions and breakouts; setting and meeting a personal goal (such as listening more actively or being open to opposing views); supplementing your course work with outside readings and discussions; helping a classmate understand the readings; peer-critiquing a classmate's work; or any other contribution to our class learning community.

Even if your professors don't define course engagement this way (or discuss it at all), boosting your engagement with course materials and conversations can have many benefits beyond the class participation grade. Engagement helps professors get to know you (and write meaningful recommendation letters). It helps you achieve other learning objectives, such as understanding the material and expressing yourself using the terms and standards of your academic discipline.

What Is Class Time For?

We all might take for granted that courses include class meetings (although some online classes don't). Why we have class meetings often goes unsaid—but it shouldn't. The purpose of instructional time varies by course, discipline, and professor. In large lecture classes student participation beyond attendance is seldom required or assessed. In smaller courses, discussion can help students achieve or demonstrate course learning goals.

In my classes, I explain that my sense of class time is connected to the value of inquiry and loving the questions. I then ask students to add their ideas. My vision for class time reflects that my courses are small (under forty students) and designed to get students thinking and talking about complex texts, laws, and policies. It also reflects an aspiration that I believe many faculty share—to create a space where people are trying to love hard questions, and where they see one another as collaborators worthy of respect, encouragement, and honesty.

Is Class Time for Debate? (It Depends)

One popular critique of contemporary campus discourse is that there is insufficient debate.[1] This critique, heard generously, can describe students' hesitation to disagree with one another for fear of causing offense or experiencing social consequences for being an outlier. A restorative mindset—in which education is the natural consequence of good-faith errors—should diminish any such fears.

Nonetheless, the idea that college course time is for actual debate—positional combat among opposing ideas—is not fully accurate. Rather than aiming for civil debate (fighting kindly) students most often engage in discussion or robust constructive dialogue. Unlike debate, dialogue is collaborative, with participants working toward shared understanding.[2]

1. Aaron R. Hanlon, "Have the Founders of the University of Austin Been in a Classroom Lately?" *The New Republic*, November 11, 2021, https://newrepublic.com/article/164363/university-austin-uatx-myth-illiberalism.

2. Based on "Comparing Debate, Discussion and Dialogue," a handout developed by Ratnesh Nagda, Patricia Gurin, Jaclyn Rodriguez, and Kelly Maxwell (2008) for the Program on Intergroup Relations, Conflict and Community (IGRC), University of Michigan, https://depts.washington.edu/fammed/wp-content/uploads/2018/06/3d-HANDOUT.pdf.

Here are some of the types of communication that can take place in a class:

- Dialogue: multiple sides or perspectives contribute their ideas with the understanding that other participants' reactions and feedback can help improve them.
- Discussion: people offer many ideas into a space to build community, seek clarity, improve comprehension, or start to develop positions.
- Debate: opponents attempt to prove one another wrong, sometimes for an audience.
- Critique: offering a judgment on a work or statement, usually using an agreed-upon standard.

A conversation can be a dialogue even when there is strong disagreement. In fact, as you build your skills in dialogue, and as you and your classmates develop trust and community together, your comfort with expressing principled disagreement should grow. This might prepare you to engage in debates—structured arguments between opposing sides, but that is not necessarily the end goal of a course.

Good academic writing will reflect the writer's engaging in dialogue. Examples of dialogue embedded in a paper include passages engaging with opposing, limiting, or alternative arguments or proposals; a precise thesis that includes limitations that result from dialogue with opposing ideas; and reviews of relevant research and literature.

There will also be times when class time is more of a discussion, in which students are building comprehension and forming opinions. This can include sharing personal experience with the material, establishing the extent of students' knowledge of the concepts, and brainstorming areas for further inquiry. A dialogue in which you present your positions and use each other's feedback to amend, strengthen, or change them is the next step.

Let's apply these ideas: Discussion, dialogue, debate, or critique?

1. Students present their business plans to a panel of local business owners. The panelists ask questions and fill out feedback forms that apply principles of marketing, finance, and management to each business plan.
2. The professor assigns *The Apology of Socrates*. In class, he asks students to identify the major ideas and concepts in the reading. As a class, the professor and students explore the reading and consider some questions about what it means.
3. After students read *The Apology of Socrates*, the professor asks the class "Under what circumstances is it acceptable to punish a teacher for corrupting youth?" One student offers an idea, and subsequent students provide alternatives or variations.
4. The professor splits the class into two groups. They are given a model law that empowers parents to sue schools for teaching age-inappropriate material. Group 1 is assigned to argue in support of the new law. Group 2 is assigned to argue against it. After 20 minutes of small group work, the professor asks each group to make their case, hear the other side's argument, and refute one another's points.[3]

3. Answers: 1 critique; 2 discussion; 3 dialogue; 4 debate.

Communicating to Be Understood: A Framework for Collaboration

Pivoting from combat to collaboration means we are all in this together—and we want our colleagues and collaborators to succeed. This section is not a guide to what you are allowed to say or even what you should say. That would be inconsistent with the goal of this text (and education itself), which is to get you thinking about how to use your expressive freedom and powers of inquiry consistent with your values and goals. This is a set of habits and practices that you can draw upon when communicating to be understood as part of the process of inquiry or problem solving.

In my experience, when people adopt these practices, conversations become more welcoming of everyone. Hateful rhetoric seldom survives a commitment to truth. Personal attacks don't happen in situations where we commit to speak for ourselves, not others. Misinformation withers upon close inquiry. This doesn't mean, however, that a commitment to speaking responsibly leads to "bubbles" or that it blunts inquiry. Imagine the following communication tools like the scales and chords you learn in your introduction to music course. Infinite musical compositions are possible when utilizing the keys, modes, or other tonal frameworks you have studied (and sometimes, whether for artistic or activist purposes, you might make the intentional choice to abandon them).

Establish Shared Understanding: Scope and Topic

In combative communication, changing the subject or conflating one topic with another is a common tactic. In fact, in my role as a political communication adviser, I advised people that when talking to the press, they should make sure their own message gets across, even if that means answering the question they want to answer rather than the one that was asked. This is especially true when the questioning is hostile and questions are framed to trap the subject or distort the truth.

A classroom should not function like a hostile press interview. When we are collaborating, participants share responsibility for determining the scope of a conversation. In classes, a professor will often present the question for discussion. If they do, it's a good practice to respond in good faith, before asking to go in a new direction or explaining why a different framing might be better. But in more open-ended discussions or dialogues, participants will have to agree at least on what is being disputed and what the question presented is. This is important because talking past one another isn't dialogue at all. We can only provide useful feedback on what we understand; we are only in dialogue if we are being responsive to one another.

Make a practice of checking for understanding both when you are offering ideas and when you are responding to them. Making sure that we are all in the same conversation—and that everyone understands what is being said—helps avoid disputes based on misunderstanding and maintain the structural integrity of a conversation. Trained dialogue facilitators and mediators (neutral parties who facilitate dispute resolution) employ a technique called "mirroring" to ensure all parties have a shared understanding of what's being said. When mirroring, you state your impression of what is being said and check to see if that matches the speaker's intention. Here are some examples of mirroring to establish understanding and the scope of the conversation:

- I think you are asking whether I agree or disagree with the author's main argument. Do I have that right?
- If I'm understanding correctly, we're discussing how we would implement this idea, not whether we should. Is that your understanding?

When checking for understanding, listen for feedback. People might disagree with your understanding about what's been said. This is an opportunity for participants in a dialogue to explore their topic's complexity. You might find, in checking for understanding, that multiple approaches to the issue are possible.

Establishing Understanding: Operational Definitions

In addition to establishing shared understanding about the scope and nature of your conversation, it is helpful to establish shared operational definitions[4] of key terms. This is particularly true when we speak about issues relating to deeply personal and important human experiences and wade into territory that is fertile for dispute. A conversation in which parties

4. "Operational Definition," American Psychological Association Dictionary of Psychology, https://dictionary.apa.org/operational-definition (accessed June 16, 2023).

make claims based on an unstable, varied, or undefined term will be unlikely to lead to greater shared understanding. Do not assume your conversation partners share your sense of what a term comprehends. This is important when a term could encompass a wide variety of things. For example, the term "religious" could refer to belief in a higher being, regularly attending religious services, or any number of different religious practices. Being explicit about how you will define a term avoids confusion.

In my areas of study, I often see terms related to partisanship and ideology used with shifting or nonexistent definitions, leading to confusing and unproductive dialogue. To be more precise, use "Republican" and "Democrat" to describe partisan affiliation. When you say "conservative," "liberal," and "moderate" you are describing ideological categories—which themselves have shifting meanings over time and depending upon context. I have found that students and even professional writers and journalists sometimes use these terms interchangeably, which muddies conversations. Leaning heavily on ideological categories (liberal, moderate, conservative) without defining them also leads to imprecise conversations—and writing.

Take, for example, political writing that describes mistrust of the 2020 election results as "conservative." This does not connect with the dictionary definition of conservatism nor the tradition of political conservatism as practiced in the United States. It describes a partisan viewpoint in a particular moment. Sloppy use of common terms tends to spill over into popular conversation—including college classrooms. But because college dialogue is about communicating to be understood, it's important to avoid slipping into this kind of generalization.

Using terms with greater precision also helps remind participants in a dialogue that individuals remain free to form positions through inquiry and that partisan or ideological identity need not dictate their position.

When you introduce an idea, define your terms, and avoid generalized terms as stand-ins for more useful data points. This practice is closely connected to the college norm of making provable (objective) claims. When your term is undefined, it is hard to make a provable claim about it.

Consider the claim "left-wingers support abolishing the death penalty." What is a "left-winger?" Is there an objective line that separates left-wingers from everyone else? Dispensing with "left-winger" and replacing it with a more objectively provable descriptor, such as "people who self-identify as very liberal" or "people who supported Bernie Sanders in 2020" enables us to have a reasoned conversation and avoid generalizations that lead to confusion.

The word "radical" is also used in multiple and contradictory ways that can impair understanding. It can be a relative term, describing an idea's proximity to what the median person believes. For example, in the ninteeenth century, "Radical Republicans" opposed slavery—a position that is currently almost universal (and codified in our constitution). Using radical as a relative term, cannabis legalization was "radical" in the 1990s—but not today.

Radical can also mean contrary to the fundamental nature of our society. For example, a proposal to require religious tests for public office in the United States would be radical even if popular because it is both unconstitutional and contrary to core values of pluralism.

Each meaning of the word "radical" expresses a completely different critique and value. An idea's unpopularity can be unrelated to its merit. Use "radical" with precision (or better yet, try more descriptive terms).

The Most Misused and Abused Word

For such a little word, "we" makes a lot of trouble. Sometimes, the definition is obvious. For example, if I say "we" are going to discuss *Texas v. Johnson* in class on Tuesday, my students know who "we" refers to. What if I say, "*we* are better than this?" How about "*we* never saw this coming?" The definition depends on context. For example, if I'm a structural engineer holding a press conference about a building collapse, *we* would likely mean me and my team. But sometimes *we* will represent a statement—intentional or otherwise—of exclusion. For example, a writer claimed that until Instagram, *we* didn't know how the ultra-wealthy lived. Commenters rightly pointed out that extremely wealthy people usually employ household workers, and that the author defined "we" to implicitly exclude these workers (who were likely to be poor and nonwhite).

We can be deployed to convert the usual to the universal. For example, at my college, I have sometimes corrected students who use it to refer to Democrats and liberals. It's true that AU students are more likely to be left of center, but it's not universal. I've also been in rooms where *we* means Christians, people who don't have disabilities, or conservatives—to name a few. An imprecisely used "we" can be a signal of who you think belongs or who you believe matters at all.

I recommend using "we" with care. Take the time to define the "we" in your claim, and think about whether, when speaking in a group, you really mean everyone or a defined group of people, such as Democrats, Christians, citizens, students, people with wealth, white people, or Americans.

Deploy Evidence with Integrity and Precision

A deceptively hard quiz:

Which of the following is evidence?

a. Polar bears are white.
b. A CDC study concluded that monosodium glutamate does not cause migraines.
c. Ted Cruz loves Nickelback.

When I show this on a slide in class, hands shoot up immediately. *It's b! Obviously, it's b!*

Not so fast. It's true that option b looks most like the kind of credible source that you might find cited in a paper. But none of these is evidence, because evidence is something more than information; it is information with a relationship to a specific claim.

What if my claim is "Ted Cruz is a Canadian Gen Xer?" The CDC study can't help us there; polar bears' color is irrelevant. Option c, if true, could potentially help us prove our claim. What would we need to know in order to know whether Ted Cruz really loves Nickelback? What would we need to know to determine whether this data point[5] helps prove our claim?

Our exercise illustrates a few important points about evidence, which is the information we use to support our claims and ideas. First, evidence doesn't exist in a vacuum. An iron skillet hanging in your kitchen is not "evidence" on its own. But it could become evidence if it is found at a crime scene where the victim suffered blunt force trauma. Or, for a less sinister example, it could serve as evidence for the claim that you cook homemade meals.

Deploying evidence with integrity means more than determining whether a source is credible. It means ensuring there is a connection between your data point and the claim you are making and respecting the limitations of what it can be used to mean. Continuing with our skillet example, your skillet can be used as evidence that you are a cook (particularly if it shows signs of use and nobody else has access to your kitchen). However, it cannot serve as evidence that Americans are cooking more or that Gen Z killed the restaurant business.

Understand the Difference between Illustrative Examples and Anecdotal Evidence

Telling a story that illustrates your claim in practice is a great tool for communicating to be understood. For example, when I teach about expressive conduct, I ask students to think about

5. I don't know if Senator Cruz (R-TX) actually likes Nickelback.

the difference between kneeling in protest and kneeling to tie your shoe. Illustrative examples help readers and listeners understand what you mean or how your idea would work in practice. Put another way, if your idea or rule is a car, an illustrative example is a test drive. If your claim is a machine, an illustrative example lets the reader (or listener) turn it on and see how it works. Illustrative examples can make your writing clearer, more accessible, and more persuasive.

Deploying an individual example to prove a general point is different. "Jeremy told me to shut up" is an anecdote. It can serve as an illustration of speech that is protected in the public square but violates classroom norms of civility. It *cannot* prove your claim that "Ohio State students don't believe in free speech." Effective writers and communicators know the difference between using a story to illustrate versus using one to prove a broad claim.

When crafting an argument, whether in class or in writing, look closely at the materials you plan to use for evidence. Consider what they can prove and what still remains to be learned. Class time can provide an excellent opportunity to fill those gaps and find out what other information would enable you to make your claim.

Learn Disciplinary Standards for Argumentation and Sources

Like "evidence," relevance and even credibility depend upon context. As you've learned, no amount of information can overcome the legal conclusion that a toddler can't consent to a contract. Therefore, in a conversation about whether a contract can be enforced, evidence that a specific child has extraordinary maturity and intellect would not be relevant. But in a conversation about whether a child was ready to read young adult fiction, this evidence might be relevant and probative.

As you pursue course work in a variety of disciplines, pay close attention to the types of questions your discipline asks and the kinds of sources that are used to answer them. You will not only learn to listen and read like a practitioner of your discipline, but to write and reason like one as well. You will find that even the term "truth" can mean different things depending upon your discipline or the argument you are having. For example, your biology exam might include true/false questions about physical processes or phenomena. But in other disciplines (such as philosophy) you will find resistance to the idea that there is only one stable truth, even when there is no dispute about underlying facts.

Disciplinary standards are constructs; they were created by human beings. This means that while it is helpful to be literate about disciplinary standards, robust college-level inquiry also invites us to question these standards—including when it comes to evaluating sources. For example, if it is well established that published studies focus more on one part of the population than another, then it is possible that excluding stories of lived experience—particularly from those who are left out of the research—makes our inquiry less useful and truthful. We should consider disciplinary norms as useful for structuring conversation and inquiry, but not as sacred and immune to questioning.

Centering Your Audience

Ask most any writer or writing teacher their best advice, and they will most likely say some variation on "understand your audience."[6] This is also true for speaking, whether in a classroom or elsewhere.

"Writer-based prose" is the opposite of that. It is a term writing instructors use for writing that makes sense to the author but does not connect with an audience.[7] Class notes, journals, and other texts we write for ourselves are often writer-based. First drafts often contain writer-based prose. This is a normal part of the writing process. Thoughts that originate in our minds are going to be more clear to us than to an outsider—much like the jokes and language we share with friends are accessible to a few select people but hard for strangers or mere acquaintances to understand. Often people who consider themselves to be "bad" writers are simply writers in progress, learning to translate their inside thought processes to outside audiences.

When producing assignments such as papers and presentations, you can turn your drafts to more audience-based prose by seeking peer input (consistent with academic integrity rules). If peer review isn't feasible for you (or sounds scary), you can also try reading your drafts aloud. This practice enables you to assume the role of listener and author at the same time.

6. "Know Your Audience," Skills You Need, https://www.skillsyouneed.com/write/know-your-audience.html (accessed June 16, 2023).

7. Linda Flower, "Writer-Based Prose: A Cognitive Basis for Problems in Writing," *College English* 41, no. 1 (September 1979): pp. 19–37.

Kindness

It's possible to center one's audience and still be unkind. After all, some audiences enjoy cruelty to their imagined enemies. I leave it to you to consider under what circumstances you want to support or produce that kind of message. In a dialogue, however, our goal is to be understood. This includes concern for the audience.

Communication Should Be Accessible and Respectful

Accessibility

Everyone in the target audience should have full and equal access to your message. The simplest accessibility step we can take is not to assume universal knowledge of matters that are not in the course readings (or covered by prerequisites). When making a cultural or historical reference not covered by the course, consider whether it will be familiar to everyone. Check for understanding and be ready to explain.

Practice accessibility in what you share as well. This means familiarizing yourself with accessibility features such as alt text (descriptions of pictures and graphs in your websites and presentations); captioning (for videos); and accessible text formats (for PDFs and printed materials). Making a habit of using accessibility features all of the time takes the burden of requesting alternatives or accommodations off of the people who use them. Practicing accessibility can also save you time. Many colleges now have policies against sharing materials that are inaccessible. So if you want your college to share your movie, website, or presentation, it will have to be accessible.

New college writers often use flowery language and complex sentence structures, believing this is what academic writing is supposed to look like. Some academic writing is complex, but complexity is not the goal. Strive to be understandable. I often ask students to read their drafts aloud. If you can't get through a sentence without taking a breath, there's a good chance your reader will find it hard to understand.

Respect for Autonomy

Volumes have been written about how to be inclusive in a diverse community. It's likely that your college will offer programming during orientation or first-year seminars to explore your rights and responsibilities as a community member. As you now know, school rules about inclusive communication can vary somewhat. In the context of a good-faith dialogue, respectful communication means, at least, following people's lead about how to refer to them. If your classmate introduces himself as Matthew, don't assume you're invited to call him Matt. If your professor refers to herself as autistic, I guarantee she's aware that "person with autism" is an available description and has not chosen it. You can expect this kind of respect from people too. For example, if your name is uncommon at your school, you can insist people don't shorten it for their convenience. But if a classmate wants to use a shortened or anglicized name in class, that is their choice to make.

Be Informed

A good-faith dialogue, where everyone is presumed to be acting in good faith, depends upon participants' taking their responsibilities seriously. This means preparing for class by doing the reading and preparing for your learning community by making an effort to understand the perspectives around you. Recall that a good-faith presumption can disproportionately burden some people (particularly those who are underrepresented in the student body). Pay close attention to how people refer to themselves and the boundaries they set. Remember: you will likely learn more from your classmates than from your professors, but your classmates aren't obligated to teach you—like you, they came to college to learn.

Accept Feedback with Gratitude—Even if You Don't Fully Get It

In a college classroom, all participants benefit from a presumption of good faith, and this includes when they are offering criticisms or expressing that they have been hurt. In a restorative environment where learning, not punishment, is the consequence of our mistakes, we can be grateful when people have been honest about how we're making them feel. As a professor, I try to model this gratitude for my students—even though being corrected in front of thirty people can feel awkward.

You don't have to understand (or agree with) someone's point of view to take their feedback at face value. Let's say in a class presentation, you say "our idea is like bacon—it makes everything better!" One student offers that this metaphor excludes students who observe Kosher or Halal dietary practices. Maybe you believe the statement was sufficiently inclusive because it implicitly includes vegetarian bacon substitutes. Or perhaps you don't know much about Jewish or Muslim dietary rules but didn't mean to leave anyone out. You can take the feedback now and make a note to learn later. This also applies to other ways one might self-identify, such as their gender. Whether you relate to a student's identity or not, practice respecting that other people are the experts on themselves (and know that you are the number one expert on you).

Understand the Difference between Productive and Unproductive Discomfort

If I had a nickel for every time someone told me "College is about being uncomfortable," I could probably retire. Of course, no one who says this means it would be better if college students took their exams in unheated buildings filled with toxic black mold. Under what circumstances, then, is discomfort beneficial to the college experience?

Generally, when people describe discomfort as a positive in college, they mean having one's ideas challenged or struggling to master a new competency. It can be productive to learn that what we were taught in high school is incomplete—even though this knowledge might be alarming or uncomfortable. But being belittled or degraded would not benefit our education and could make it harder to learn. It would also be impossible to have good-faith discussions if anyone's subjective sense of offense constituted a reason to punish. What we can do is try—and be open to discussing why some conversations are particularly burdensome.

Apologize with Integrity

Small children can be forced to apologize (what would we need to know in order to determine whether it's a good idea to make them do so?); in an adult learning community, choosing to apologize is a way to build relationships of trust and move on from hard moments. But apologizing insincerely or going through the motions of apology without showing understanding is a recipe for further distrust and hurt.

Even though I believe in expressive freedom, sometimes I wish I could waive a magic wand and make three pesky phrases go away. Of course, I can't do that, but I do want to make my case for why you should consider shelving them too, as they make all kinds of mischief. They are:

Just my opinion

Sorry, but . . .

and

Sorry if you are (offended, hurt)

These phrases I find so mischievous are all methods of avoiding responsibility for one's speech. In a way, they are the worst of both worlds, representing a decision neither to self-edit out of kindness or tact, nor to fully stand behind what you've said. Deployed in a contentious conversation, they can be a way of avoiding apology, even when using the same word as a real apology ("sorry").

Just My Opinion

"Just my opinion" is an easy alternative to offering evidence in circumstances when the speaker acknowledges that the claim is contentious, and evidence would help. If you find yourself feeling tempted to say "just my opinion," ask yourself—why do I need to say this? If it's because some evidence is needed, an alternative is to pivot to inquiry and acknowledge uncertainty; I'm not actually sure of this position. It's my instinct, but it could be wrong. What would we need to know to verify it? Can you help me see what I am missing?

If you are saying "just my opinion" because you know what you are saying is potentially hurtful, it's useful to ask yourself why you are planning to say it, and whether your statement needs to be said—rather than offering a defensive disclaimer. Finally, if you are saying "just my opinion" to blunt someone else's defensiveness, or because you do not feel other parties to the conversation are going to take your point well, it might be worthwhile to consider whether more groundwork needs to be laid before you are ready to discuss this issue with this group. Is there a power imbalance that prevents you from being forthright with them? Are they not listening generously? Do they have some reason to mistrust you?

Sorry, but . . .

If I were a gambler, I'd bet that no kind and productive comment has ever come from a sentence that began with "sorry, but . . ." On the contrary, it is often an opening parry into an insult:

Sorry, but you're crazy if you think that's going to work.

Sorry, but she looked ridiculous up there.

If you've ever been on the receiving end of a "sorry, but" statement, you probably didn't experience the speaker as being truly sorry, or even sympathetic.

If "sorry, but" is on the tip of your tongue, this might be a circumstance where normative self-editing is in order. Ask yourself: What are you sorry for? The hurt you are about to inflict? The unfortunate truth you believe you are about to share?

Recall the distinction between subjective and objective (provable) claims. If your "sorry, but" is followed by a subjective claim ("sorry, but she is just not the best public speaker"), it could be helpful to interrogate why you believe your subjective assessment—which you are verbally acknowledging is hurtful—is needed. If, on the other hand, you are making an objective claim ("sorry, but Southern High School's test scores are the lowest in the county"), it could be helpful to consider why you are making a pro forma apology about it. Is it because your intention in sharing the objective fact is to denigrate someone? Is there a more productive alternative that would not require a preemptive apology?

Sorry If You Were Offended

Saying "sorry if" is a way to shift responsibility away from yourself and onto the listener, who becomes responsible for imagining the injury. In the workshops on apology I facilitate, participants have the strongest negative reactions to "sorry if" apologies, agreeing that they are worse than no apology at all.

In some contexts—such as when admitting wrong can lead to punishment—defensively avoiding responsibility for harm is understandable, if not admirable. But in a restorative context, where participants have an opportunity to build their competencies based on constructive dialogue, avoiding responsibility is not so rational. Listening generously—including to our critics—sometimes means accepting feedback about our impact on others, even if that surprises us. When we try receiving this kind of feedback with gratitude, we also pave the way for the people around us to try to keep communicating with us.

Instead of avoiding responsibility or making a false apology, I recommend apologizing with integrity. Apologizing with integrity means apologizing when you are actually sorry to have caused harm, rather than inflicting hurt and using a throw-away phrase as a shield or negotiating to a middle ground where you acknowledge harm but not your role in it.

Sometimes, though, you really aren't sorry. If you have honestly engaged with good faith critique or claim of harm and still believe it missed the mark, it is more honest—and therefore more useful to the other person—to state, "I genuinely don't understand what went wrong here," or "I see you are upset, but I do feel what I said was valid." Insincerity, by contrast, can erode trust even more than declining to apologize at all.

Productive Discourse beyond the Classroom

A core function of expressive freedom is to enable active, engaged citizenship. Although dialogue in college will vary in significant ways from community engagement and activism (for example, in a classroom no one is necessarily trying to "win"), you can still apply the concepts here to your dialogue and inquiry beyond the classroom. Whether you want to heal the world or make your college more responsive to student concerns, your powers of inquiry and expression will serve you. Here are some points on communicating to make change.

Understand the Institutions You Are Seeking to Change

When I was in law school, I didn't want to take an elective course on corporations. A wise senior lawyer with a distinguished career in civil rights law told me, "You can't sue them if you don't know how they work." I am very glad I took a class on corporations, which enabled me to do a wide variety of interesting work I did not even imagine when I enrolled. The underlying advice—to understand the institutions you wish to change—has proven true for me time and again.

Understand the institutions you want to change with the degree of detail that the characters in a jewel heist movie understand their target. It's particularly important to understand what each target of your activism is capable of doing. What authority do they have? What barriers to exercising it do they possess? What committees, funding sources, and programs do they manage? When does their budget year end? To whom do they report? Understanding an institution is essential to deciding what you can ask for, and whom you need to ask. It is also essential if you want to craft accurate public criticisms. If you criticize a powerful institution but you are wrong about the facts, the moral weight of your cause can get lost in the shuffle.

Know Your Goals and Communicate Them Clearly

Once you understand the institution (whether university or city hall) you are petitioning, you can decide what to ask for. It's important to be able to describe what you are hoping to accomplish. Your anger or passion will motivate you, but it will not necessarily engage the people you're petitioning, nor hold the greater community's attention without an action item. Always, always have an ask that you can explain clearly.

Understand That Changing Minds Is a Kind of Progress (the Overton Window)

Sometimes your goal will be to change minds so you can change policies or laws further down the road. There is a term called the "Overton window"[8] that describes the limitations of current possible policy outcomes. Advocates for major social change often focus on moving the Overton window, so

8. "The Overton Window," Mackinac Center for Public Policy, https://www.mackinac.org/OvertonWindow (accessed June 16, 2023).

that proposals currently seen as radical or impossible today become mainstream in the future. Examples of the Overton window moving in recent history include the movement for marriage equality for same-sex couples, which saw a massive shift in support in the early 2000s; and the movement to legalize cannabis possession and use, which gained popular support even more recently.

Changing minds demands a different type of communication than changing the rules. While changing the rules requires understanding levers of power, changing minds requires trust, extended dialogue, and persuasion—which require understanding the people in your community. When I was working as a legislative advocate, I was tasked with communicating with a wide variety of audiences. This demands humility and patience; we aren't the ones who will decide which of our points is most persuasive—that is for the listeners to decide.

An example of what I mean: in the early 2000s, I worked in a coalition opposing a proposed amendment to the US Constitution that would have barred same-sex couples from marrying or receiving the legal benefits and protections of marriage. Many in the coalition (including me) believed the strongest argument related to the distinction between civil marriage (a legal status conferred by government) and the religious sacrament of marriage (a ceremony or rite recognized by a faith community). We wanted to emphasize that the government cannot require religious communities to change their rules for religious marriage—regardless of what rules it sets for civil marriage. This was an accurate point, and most of the lawyers I worked with assumed it would be quite compelling.

But opinion research showed us that this message did not persuade the target audience, and that certain other messages were much more effective.

It can be hard to pivot away from what we feel is our strongest argument (it's especially hard for lawyers to hear that the legal argument isn't the strongest one). Ultimately, though, the question whether an argument is compelling is for the audience to decide. That is one more reason it's beneficial to build our skills at accepting feedback and become more responsive to audience preferences. The First Amendment (and related policies) ensure we are not punished for our viewpoints, but they cannot help us win hearts or minds or achieve our goals in a democratic and diverse society.

Productivity, Professional Goals, and Your Public Voice

The decision not to speak—or to select your words with care—isn't always a bad one. Sometimes these decisions reflect a concern for consequences beyond grades or freedom. Our way of speaking is how people come to know us, and as architects of that image, it's on each of us to present ourselves consistent with professional and personal goals—and understanding that others are free to draw their own conclusions from what we say.

For most of the history of higher education, few college students graduated with a visible record of public statements. But since many college students now have a presence on social media, even "private" people now have a traceable public image.

The decision whether, when, and how to speak up has become more consequential since the development of technology that publishes nearly anyone and remembers everything.

If you attend a public university, or one that has a strong free expression policy, your protected online speech should be like protected speech on the campus quad. Assuming you are not harassing or threatening anyone, your choice to express yourself, including disagreement with others, is yours to make. Because social media platforms are private entities, they might choose to label misinformation or punish speech that violates their terms—but that is between you and the platform, not your university.

Speech can also have consequences besides official punishment (and beyond campus). Potential employers, graduate schools, and social and community organizations—in addition to friends and other members of your campus community—are free to form judgments and make decisions based on your online speech. It has become common for employers to review job applicants' social media activity, for example.[9] Private entities (including future employers) may engage in viewpoint discrimination and punish speech, such as by declining to hire students who have a visible record of combative or vulgar online speech or expression, or whose online persona is inconsistent with their image, positions, or business model.

I'm not advising against being passionate or opinionated online. When you focus on what you want for yourself—which

9. David Cotriss, "Keep It Clean: Social Media Screenings Gain in Popularity," Business News Daily, August 5, 2022, https://www.businessnewsdaily.com/2377-social-media-hiring.html.

could include a successful postcollege job search—you might conclude that your online voice and image needs to reflect those goals. Many career advisers will encourage you to do the same.

If the idea of curtailing what you express to avoid angering an as-yet unspecified employer doesn't sound like your idea of "free" speech, you've got a point. If students and faculty have expressive freedom online regardless of whether our universities disagree with what we say, why should that end when we leave school and start work? You might believe that it should not—and some people will agree with you.

Managing Hot Moments: Tailoring Communication to Your Goals in the Moment

Just as your long-term goals can shape your decision about the kind of public or online voice you share, so your shorter-term goals can help you decide how you use your voice in a particular moment. In academic spaces, a primary goal is being understood. This is different from some other contexts. For example, political candidates often communicate to promote an image of themselves, persuade people to take action, to illustrate the difference between them and the other candidate, or even to shame the other side—also a common feature of online discourse. Online, we might communicate with the intention of getting attention, "owning" a perceived opposing group, or for a laugh.

Often, online speech has no clear purpose. Twitter is not a legislature; we don't gather there to plan community responses to pressing problems. We might be there to pass the time, to find people who are angry at the same things we are, and in some cases to find out the news—or what our favorite and least favorite people think of the news.

Applying an ethos of purposiveness to online discussion might seem frustrating or fruitless. After all, online spaces can be filled with bad-faith actors, trolls, and willful peddlers of misinformation. But whether online or in a residence hall lounge, ultimately you are the person looking out for yourself and keeping your goals, reputation, and resources (including emotional reserves) in mind. It can be helpful, particularly when you find yourself in heated conversations, to take a beat, ask what you want for yourself out of this conversation, and plan your speech accordingly.

Discussion Questions and Classroom Exercises for Chapter 5

- *What is class time for*? Faculty may choose to share their own list and encourage students to create theirs, as on this table, taken from a slide I share on the first day of class:

My list	Your list
• Trying	• ________________
• Making mistakes	• ________________
• Listening	• ________________
• Improving	• ________________
• Struggling	• ________________
• Having fun	• ________________
• Pushing one another to refine ideas	• ________________

- *Operational definitions*: Are there terms in this field of study that we need to define? What are they? Attempt to define one or more of these commonly used terms:
  - Bias/biased
  - Hurtful/hateful
  - Neutral
  - Fair
  - Violent/violence
- Information literacy: Incorporate a research librarian presentation into the course or have students utilize library research training resources.
- Consider the methods and disciplinary standards that apply in your major field of study (or in the discipline associated with this course). What rules and norms make sense to you? Which ones seem archaic, unfair, or hard to understand?
- Sometimes participants in a dialogue will say that progress is slow and call for patience. How can we use the concept of the Overton window to transform a call for patience into a process of collaborative inquiry?
- Practice responding to feedback and offering clarifications. Pairs of students take turns explaining a complex concept to one another (e.g., the infield fly rule from baseball; how to braid a loaf of challah; photosynthesis). Listeners ask clarifying questions or indicate when they don't understand. Speakers practice clarification, checking for understanding, and rephrasing.

Writing Exercises for Chapter 5

- *Information literacy:* Familiarize yourself with your library's research tools, online or in person. Practice structuring a research question on a topic of interest to you. Find academic resources on the subject. Create a literature review or annotated bibliography.
- *Operational definitions*: Define a term that is relevant to the course. Explain what it means and provide examples of how it works in practice.
- *Illustrative examples versus anecdotal evidence*: Read an opinion piece that includes one or more anecdotes. Identify and discuss how these anecdotes are being used—as illustrative examples or as anecdotal evidence. Discuss how this affects the argument's strength and persuasiveness. Research the claim the anecdote is used to support. What did you find? How could the opinion writer have bolstered their argument with data?
- *The Overton window*: Consider a public policy matter that is important to you. Describe the current spectrum of possible legislation and discussion on this matter. Has this spectrum of possibility and discussion changed since you started paying attention to it? In your lifetime?

6

Where Do I Fit?

ENGAGE IN SELF-REFLECTION

> Being the architect of your voice means actively deciding how best to communicate in service of your goals and values; taking responsibility for your choices as a member of the university community; pushing yourself to engage in rigorous inquiry; and challenging yourself to make the most of your education.[1]

AT THE BEGINNING of every semester, I ask my students to consider two big questions:

What do you want for yourself?

What will you ask of yourself?

The two questions with which I begin each semester reflect two pillars of civic dialogue: liberty and community. The

1. "Building My Voice," Project on Civil Discourse, American University, School of Public Affairs, https://www.american.edu/spa/civic-dialogue/building-my-voice.cfm (accessed September 7, 2023).

choice to pursue an education reflects a commitment to yourself: meeting your goals, expanding your opportunities, building your life. Reflecting on why you are in college (or in the class where you're reading this book) and what you hope to achieve there is the first step to knowing how you will use your expressive and academic freedom.

Meeting your goals requires individual commitment and sacrifice—of time, tuition money, often proximity to family or old friends. Reflecting on your individual strengths and challenges prepares you to meet more specific goals. If you want to become a journalist or artist, for example, and you know you are defensive about constructive feedback, then you have some work to do because studio art courses often include peer critique and even top journalists get feedback from editors (and increasingly from the public).

Pursuing a college education also means joining a community where you are one among many voices. You will share space in classrooms, on shuttle buses, in dining halls, and (if you go away to school) in the residence halls. You will need to build your skills both as an individual and as a community member taking on a new set of challenges. The communal nature of college and of communication itself requires us to look beyond ourselves, dig deep, and commit to hard work.

To know what you will need to ask of yourself as the architect of your college education, it's helpful to explore what the enterprise of college (and civic) dialogue is all about, what can make it challenging, and how that might differ from simplistic popular descriptions of "campus free speech wars."

The concept of "productive" discourse is inherently linked to one's goals. If one's goal is to entertain a crowd, comedy is productive. If one's goal is to get people to immediately run for safety, shouting is productive. To understand what constitutes a productive use of your time in college, first consider why you're there.

Why Am I in College?

Pursuing a college education can earn you a credential that helps secure a job. It can be a time to explore, perhaps for the first time, life away from parents and family. It can be a way to learn skills you'll need to live your life, pursue a career, or be the kind of friend, sibling, neighbor, spouse, parent, or citizen that you want to be. Maybe you're passing time in college because people expected you to; that doesn't mean you cannot find a purpose of your own that propels you. College can also be a place to explore questions and ideas for the joy of it. In my experience, students who find joy in learning—and seek out courses that truly interest them—are more likely to build their skills and achieve practical goals, such as learning what type of work they might find fulfilling and improving their resilience to challenges.

Don't Project Your Own Goals onto Others

In your residence hall or class, there will be students whose idea of college dialogue will be different from yours. You might have come to college hoping for the kind of late-night philosophical debates your parents speak fondly about from their college years. But another classmate might have looked forward to college as a time to stop locking horns in combat.

No one owes you a chance to debate them nor an explanation why they won't. Nor is the decision not to engage in a debate a reflection of weakness or closed mindedness. Respect people's boundaries. And if you are seeking "debate" and not finding ready takers, try being open to other ways of engaging, such as dialogue.

If you are not sure why you're in college or what you hope to achieve there, exploring those questions might be your first task. Take some time to think of your big-picture goals, particularly as they relate to communication. Do you want to become a more effective writer or speaker? If your career and life goals are starting to take shape, consider what role communication will play. Will you have to listen to clients' concerns? Talk to patients, customers, or students? Write technical instructions for consumers? Talk to community members? Listen to focus groups? Will you be working with a team? Do you see yourself someday leading an organization or a department? If you talk to people in your chosen field, you will find that the answer is likely yes—regardless of what field you are pursuing.

Reexamining the Challenge of College Discourse—the Relationship between Self and Community

One semester, three first-year students from the same class separately made these statements to me:

> This is the most diverse school I've ever gone to.
> This is the least diverse place I've ever been.
> Until I came here, I didn't know what white people thought of us.

How can three students in the same class in the same year at the same college have such different perceptions of their campus? The answer is that each was describing their own experience of the campus and its comparison to their previous communities. They were describing a complex entity that consists not only of some objective, separate entity called "American University," but the community as they experienced it. Ask a student what they think about "college," and the answer will consist of at least these things:

- Their perception of "objective" features of the community (for example, how many students are enrolled).
- Their perception of how they are perceived in that community (an insider, an outlier, typical, or atypical).
- Their perception of how that community differs from other places they have been; and
- Their specific experience with and in the institution.[2]

As my students learned, your experience as a college student will reflect more than the school's measurable characteristics. It will not only be dependent upon your individual personality, skills, and preferences—though you should also reflect upon those. The challenge of college dialogue, for you, will also depend upon the nature of your transition to college: how the community compares to your past experiences and how ready you are for change.

2. Individuals develop a sense of self by observing how they are perceived by others. "Perception Is Reality: The Looking Glass-Self," Lesley University, https://lesley.edu/article/perception-is-reality-the-looking-glass-self (accessed June 16, 2023).

Even as members of the same small class at the same school, each of my students experienced this change differently. Their experiences illustrate an important reason why discourse in a college community requires instruction and practice. To prepare for college dialogue, I encourage you to engage in self-reflection about your relationship to your communities, including high school, your hometown, and your new campus.

Defaults, Diversity, and a Multiplicity of Campus Climates

When I was serving in a working group planning orientation and welcome activities for incoming students, a colleague said we need to take great care not to send a message that there's one typical student at our university. She was right; there is no one experience or background that should make you the right fit—or one that makes a student less welcome. Making that ideal a reality is something I think we should all work toward.

However, humans are social beings. When we arrive somewhere new, we notice the people around us, and we process whether we fit in. Do most people look like me, dress like me? Can they pronounce my name? Can I pronounce theirs? Does it feel like there is a default student here, even if they say there isn't supposed to be? Many things can be true at once—a college can try to include everyone but still seem to have an observable typical or "default" student. Often the typical student is middle-class, white, under age 30, not visibly disabled, liberal, and a native English speaker.

Being the default student often comes with the advantage of not noticing that there *is* a default student. On the other hand, students likely notice when they aren't typical for their student body. Some also notice that their identity matched that of the typical student better in high school than college or vice versa. For example, a student might observe that in high school, most of her classmates' families attended the same church. But at her college, there are multiple different faith traditions, and it seems like many people don't go to worship services regularly at all. So while it's true that there is a welcoming faith group on campus, it's also true that this student was much more typical in her high school than she is now.

Regardless of the college's policies on expression, or how open her peers are to her own life experience and values, she is experiencing a significant shift from being a default student to more of an outlier. She might still have a great deal in common with her fellow students—most especially their shared identities as college learners. But she can no longer assume the people she meets will have consumed the same media or experienced the same milestones. She will need to find new ways to connect and cannot take for granted that the shorthand she used for commonly shared experiences in high school will be understood by everyone around her in college. It might be exciting, scary, or both.

This fact pattern illustrates an aspect of campus climate that is often overlooked: that students could base their perception of how welcoming the campus is on how it compares to previous experiences. The college transition itself—particularly if it involves a change from typical to outlier—can affect both students' perceptions of campus climate and their readiness to engage in dialogue with one another.

This is one reason attempts to rate universities' openness to dialogue across difference are so challenging. One such effort rates schools based on a combination of university policies and students' reported perceptions.[3] Like my own students' assessment of "diversity" in their campus, students' subjective perceptions of how open their campus is to ideas represent a combination of factors. They can reflect a shift from being in the majority—or even supermajority—to being a dissenting viewpoint.

Comparing entire schools based on these measurements is potentially even more challenging than getting an accurate read on individual students. Let's compare two hypothetical universities to illustrate what I mean. At one institution in a "red" state, most self-identified conservative students come from counties where conservative or Republican identifying people are the overwhelming majority.[4] At another school in a "purple" state, most self-identified conservative students come from suburbs with significant populations of Democrats, Republicans, and independents. Both colleges have more self-identified liberal students than conservative ones. Both are located in a college town that is one of the most liberal localities in their state.

3. "2021 College Free Speech Rankings," Foundation for Individual Rights and Expression (FIRE), https://rankings.thefire.org/ (accessed June 16, 2023).

4. Increasingly, Americans live in hyperpolarized neighborhoods. Emily Badger, Kevin Quealy, and Josh Katz, "A Close-Up Picture of Partisan Segregation, Among 180 Million Voters," *New York Times*, March 17, 2021, https://www.nytimes.com/interactive/2021/03/17/upshot/partisan-segregation-maps.html.

The students at the first college are experiencing (at least) two transitions: the transition from high school to college and the transition from being the majority or default viewpoint in their community to being one of many viewpoints or a minority viewpoint. The students at the second college are also experiencing the high school to college transition, but they are not experiencing a transition from majority to minority viewpoint.

We could reasonably expect the first group of conservative students to have a subjective impression that their college is a more challenging place to espouse conservative views than high school—because this might be their first experience with expressing these ideas in a community where some or most people don't share them. Even if both schools have similar policies, similar ideological makeup, and similar percentages of the student body who claim to be open to new perspectives, the students' perceptions as measured by surveys could be very different—because for some students, communication across difference (or being a minority viewpoint) is a new experience. A rating based on student perceptions is measuring *something*—but that something might not be the school itself. Rather, it might measure the communities from which it draws its student body, and the extent to which the campus culture differs from those communities.[5]

5. These student perceptions can still be useful for administrators and faculty. For example, the students are surveyed on how clear their administration's support for expressive freedom is. It's important for administrators to explain and discuss the school's approach to expressive freedom and educate students about the meaning and extent of that commitment.

As my students' own voices show, students' experience with diversity—like ideology—reflects not only the external realities of the campus, but the students' identities and past experiences. Surveys about expression have frequently shown that Black students feel less protected by the First Amendment than their peers.[6] The fact that most college campuses (with the exception of historically Black colleges and universities, known as HBCUs) predominantly serve white students could be a part of the reason why. But the transition from high school to college is important here too: most Black students in the United States attend majority-Black elementary and secondary schools.[7] Their college transition, then, often includes a transition from typical student to outlier.

I hope that future research on campus climate takes this reality about the college transition into account. Researchers should ask students to identify their proximity to the median student (by identity, economic status, ideological orientation, rural/urban/suburban status, and other factors) in their high schools and home communities and on their college campus and look at how the transition itself affects individual students and their perceptions of campus climate. This will help schools better identify which perceptions are traceable to university policies or culture. It will also help drive practices and resources to better support students in mastering college discourse

6. "College Student Views on Free Expression and Campus Speech 2022," Knight Foundation, January 2022, https://knightfoundation.org/wp-content/uploads/2022/01/KFX_College_2022.pdf.

7. "Racial/Ethnic Enrollment in Public Schools," National Center for Education Statistics, May 2022, https://nces.ed.gov/programs/coe/indicator/cge/racial-ethnic-enrollment.

skills: meeting students where they are and recognizing that just as there is no typical student, there is no typical college transition.

In the meantime, students can prepare for the new challenges of college-level dialogue—wherever you come from, and wherever you study—by exploring your own experiences, habits, preferences, skills, and challenges as a listener and learner. This includes recognizing that expressing yourself as an outlier (whether that is because of your first language or cultural background, you practice a minority religion, you are among the ideological minority at school, you are a racial or ethnic minority in your community, you are LGBTQ, you are a veteran, you are a transfer student or nontraditional student, or for any other reason) can be more challenging even if the institution and the people in it are not trying to make it feel more difficult.

On the Gift of Being an Outlier—and the Dangers of Being Agreed With

At the university where I teach, most students identify as liberal. The school has a reputation as one of the most politically active and liberal universities in the country, though that image does not accurately reflect the diversity of ideas, preferences, and experiences of the students there. Nonetheless, it's true that there are fewer self-identified conservative students than liberal ones. One thing I tell my students—and that I hope you will think about too—is that it's much easier to get a great education as a conservative student at my school than as a liberal one.

You read that right.

Being agreed with is like sitting on your couch and watching TV: it feels good, but it's not always good for you.

There is some disagreement that improves our own ideas, sharpens our argumentation, and keeps us on our toes. Students who espouse unpopular positions—assuming they do so in good faith and in dialogue with their peers—get more constructive and useful feedback than those who hold more common positions. If, upon completing the reflection questions at the end of this chapter, you find that you have not had much experience in dialogue across difference, I encourage you to include that in your goals for college.

Fortunately, college is not a presidential election, and classroom discussions are not a referendum on yes/no questions that track the partisan binary. Well-designed classroom discussions explore shades of gray and make space for nuanced and varied solutions that mere partisan or ideological categories cannot describe.

Mental Health, Bandwidth, and Boundaries

Remember all those nice things I said about dialogue across difference? It's also really hard work. Sometimes it goes badly. Much like we sometimes need to watch a funny movie instead of a documentary, or just sit quietly with a friend rather than delve into painful events like a death in the family or a breakup, sometimes we are just not up for all of these otherwise lovable questions. You are the manager of your own time. There is no one on this green Earth with the power to make you debate them.

Know when you are up for a vigorous dialogue and replenish yourself when you need to. College is wonderful and I would say that overall, life is pretty wonderful too. But mental health challenges can happen any time, and I recommend thinking deeply about any changes you experience to your resilience and enthusiasm for dialogue with others. If you find yourself reacting more strongly and rebounding less quickly to challenging times than you usually would, please listen to yourself—the greatest expert ever on the important topic of you. Seek out a trusted friend or family member and get their read on whether you are burned out or worse. There are no medals or awards for finishing college without visiting the counseling center or chaplain. Your capacity to love questions tomorrow depends on taking care of yourself today.

Next, I invite you to consider how ready you are to take on these challenges, and identify the habits, experiences, strengths, and areas for development that you bring to the conversation. The reflection questions that follow were designed for you to consider individually at first. You might choose to write your responses or not. If you do decide to write your responses, I encourage you to include the date. Revisit the questions later in college and write again. You might find that as your studies continue and you explore the skills in this book, your answers could change.

Reflection Questions for Chapter 6

1. What do you want for yourself
    a. What is the purpose of college?
    b. Do you have goals for personal growth? Service? Interpersonal relationships? Career?

   c. Who do you want to make proud?
   d. How do you want to be seen in the college community?
   e. What subjects excite you?
   f. What kinds of questions, books, works of art, and experiences bring you joy?
2. Values about classroom discussion
   a. Do you thrive on dialogue, debate, or discussion?
   b. Do you prefer to listen, contribute, or a combination?
   c. When others are speaking, do you find yourself wanting to jump in and ask questions or add your thoughts?
3. Your actions in "hot" moments and in disagreement
   a. Do you tend to seek out conflicts? Avoid them?
   b. When other people disagree—in person or online—do you join in? When and why?
   c. Do you tend to "pile on" when someone expresses an unpopular view?
   d. Do you ever regret engaging in disagreement?
   e. Do you ever regret not getting involved?
4. How do you respond to constructive feedback?
   a. Are you ever defensive?
   b. Is it hard to show gratitude for feedback?
   c. Do you avoid communicating (or performing, writing, or creating art) to avoid getting feedback?
   d. What kind of feedback do you prefer?
   e. What kind of response to your communication is likely to make you quit or avoid future engagement?

5. Self and community before and in college
   a. What role, if any, does your identity as a (select a part of your identity that feels relevant here) play in how you engage in discussion, expression, or disagreement?
   b. Have you lived or attended school in a community with a wide range of religious, political, ideological, demographic, or economic differences?
   c. Do you have friends or family members with whom you disagree about matters that are very important to you?
   d. Do you have experience being an outlier in high school or your home community? For example, have you been a member of a minority demographic group, or have you been the only person of your gender or race in an activity or club?
   e. What characteristics or experiences do you have that you share with the majority of students in your college (for example, coming from in-state, speaking English as your first language)?
   f. What characteristics or experiences do you have that make you more of an outlier at college (for example, being a nontraditional student, being a parent, being from an underrepresented demographic group)?
   g. Have you engaged in activities where you've worked on your skills at listening and communicating across difference (for example, Girls or Boys State programs, debate, exchange programs, camps, friends from other schools, moving from one community to another)?

   h. Overall, how does your relationship to your college community compare with your relationship to your high school or home community?
   i. Are you in a position where you have the mental and emotional capacity to engage in challenging conversations and dialogue?
6. How comfortable are you with vulnerability?
   a. Do you find it hard to learn something new in front of other people?
   b. Has concern about how you will be perceived ever discouraged you from learning something new (such as a new language, sport, or instrument)?
   c. Is it hard for you to admit when you don't know something?
7. What are your values about education?
   a. Do you like to take risks?
   b. Are you focused on achievement?
   c. Do you like trying things you find very difficult?
   d. Do you love learning? Under what circumstances have you really loved learning something?
   e. Do you learn best by reading? Having conversations? Practice?
   f. How do you feel about rules? Do you see yourself as a rule follower?
8. How do you see fellow students?
   a. Are they collaborators? Competitors?
   b. Do you think students at your university are better prepared than you? Less prepared? About the same?
   c. Do you believe your fellow students share your goals and values for attending college?

   d. Do you feel you understand them?
   e. What goals and values do you believe you will share in common with them?
9. How do you handle challenging material?
   a. Do you find any subject matter hard to discuss?
   b. Do you feel uncomfortable around people expressing emotion? Do you feel uncomfortable showing emotion around others?
   c. Have you been told you're too sensitive? What do you think of that?
   d. Do you find yourself thinking other people are being too sensitive? If you have told someone they are being sensitive, how did that go?

I. Goals
   1. What would you say you would most like to work on as a listener, communicator, and student?
   2. What are some action items you plan to take this semester to make that happen?
   3. What is one thing you want to learn more about?
   4. What will excite you and motivate you most as you pursue your education?
   5. How can you protect the joy and excitement you feel about the things that motivate you?

ACKNOWLEDGMENTS

WHEN I WAS YOUNGER, I hated to be edited. I'd write a draft of an op ed or speech, hit "send," and await validation. I wanted to be so good at my craft, the only rational response would be "wow." But writing and revising are dialogue. And now that my professional life is about dialogue, I look forward to the conversations that make my written work better. Or maybe I have that backward. Perhaps as I've matured and become more open to receiving help and working through problems collaboratively, my career has inevitably moved toward dialogue.

Planning, writing, and revising this book has been a joy in large part because it's been an ongoing, rich dialogue. So many people helped me. It was nice to get the occasional "wow," but I have sincerely loved the pushback, the doubts, and—of course—the questions along the way.

When this project was a too-vague idea and then a too-specific outline, Andrea Malkin Brenner, Carlos Cortes, and Wanda Wigfall-Williams all helped me find my way toward a book worth writing, one that I hope reflects the complexity and importance of this topic.

The Brenner Family generously gave me a place to think and write uninterrupted, far from distractions and in beautiful surroundings.

Multiple times in the writing process I found myself straying from my goal, and writing reams of something that was probably not terrible but was definitely not the book I needed to write. Lori Brown helped me find my way back.

Conversations with David Sugerman and Randi Zimmerman helped me with the chapter on listening.

Jonathan Friedman, Neijma Celestine-Donnor, Benjamin Railton, Garrett Epps, Carlos Cortes, Andrea Malkin Brenner, Brian Hughes, Michelle Deutchman, Thomas Merrill, Kristen Shahverdian, Harsha Mudaliar, Keisuke Fujio, Silas Engel, and Emma Semaan all provided feedback on sections, chapters, or drafts.

Chanelle Bonsu, Sarah Marc-Woessner, Keisuke Fujio, and A. J. Given offered student perspectives on barriers to classroom conversation. Caleb Bates and Alicia Talamas shared their experiences with dialogue. Silas Engel created resources for teachers to connect these concepts to their courses.

Peter Dougherty helped me to envision an audience for this book and helped me identify the ideas from within my own work that most needed to be shared with that audience. Our conversations at every stage from proposal through peer review made the book better.

If I hadn't already grown up and learned to like being edited before I met Matt Rohal, I'm sure that working with him would have made me see the light. He is exceptionally skilled at helping a writer see her work from a different angle. He asked important questions and was abundantly patient in helping me find my way to an answer. I hope I can keep his example in mind when responding to student writing.

Thanks to copyeditor Anne Sanow and to the Princeton University Press team including Sydney Bartlett, Kathleen Cioffi, Alena Chekanov, David Campbell, Terri O'Prey, and Heather Hansen.

Thanks, Jay and Dave, for your abundant patience and encouragement.

Finally, I particularly want to thank the students whom I taught early on, before I had given classroom discussion even a fraction of the attention and study it deserved. Their feedback—and sometimes their silence—asked me the remarkable, lovable question that led to this book: "How do we make space for dialogue, and for one another?"

APPENDIX

Reflection Questions for Faculty

1. Demystifying college expectations
   a. Do I know how familiar my students are with college-level expectations, such as how to communicate with professors and when and how to express disagreement in or out of the classroom?
   b. Are my students familiar with concepts of freedom of expression, academic freedom, and the limitations on those concepts?
   c. Have I provided students with guidance regarding how their work will be evaluated in the course?
   d. Looking back on my own college, graduate school, apprenticeship, or training experience, was I ever surprised by or confused about what was expected?
   e. If I want students to experience uncertainty or struggle as part of the learning experience, have I told them/are they aware that this struggle is normative and expected?

   f. Have I explicitly invited students to contribute, including sharing what they wonder, not only what they know for certain?[1]
2. Establishing trust
   a. Have I told my students that they will not be graded on their beliefs or political orientation?
   b. Have I told them I am concerned about them as people?
   c. Do my students know the extent of my teacher training (if any!) in dialogue facilitation, trauma, interrupting bias, diversity, or de-escalation techniques?
   d. Am I aware of my students' concerns and preconceived ideas about campus speech, political difference, or social justice?
   e. Did we have a community standards conversation at the beginning of the class?
   f. Have we checked in about how the students are doing?
3. Building community
   a. What do I do to build community in my classroom or program?
   b. How would my students describe their relationship to one another (e.g., adversarial, competitive, collaborative, collegial)?

1. Remarks by Keisuke Fujio, in Lara Schwartz, Keisuke Fujio, Anna Given, Chanelle Bonsu, and Sarah Marc Woeesner, "The Quiet Classroom: Recognizing and Responding to Student Hesitancy to Speak Up," panel presentation at the Ann Ferren Conference, American University, Washington, DC, January 12, 2023, https://edspace.american.edu/afc/session-301.

   c. Is my classroom more about inquiry, discussion, dialogue, or debate?
   d. How do I incentivize, assess, and reward collaboration?
   e. How does my course material lend itself to collaborative inquiry?
   f. What parts of my discipline or related professions require collaboration or communication?
   g. Does my course design presume all students grew up in the United States and are familiar with US culture, school norms, and practices?[2]
4. Teaching challenging material
   a. Do my students know why I am presenting this material (e.g., aesthetic reasons, to question the material, for exposure to the canon)?
   b. Do my students know my relationship to this material (e.g., I have studied it, critiqued it, published about it, written or lectured about what makes it controversial or challenging)?
   c. Have I talked to my students about the role that challenging material plays in education and in the course?
   d. Do my students know they are free to question curricular choices and critique texts and artwork in college?
   e. Have I thought about the best context to introduce challenging materials (e.g., watch a video in class together or assign students to view independently)?

2. Remarks by Sarah Marc Woeesner, "The Quiet Classroom."

5. Managing hot moments
    a. How do I feel about highly charged or emotional conversations?
    b. Do I understand the extent of my authority to interrupt bias or set boundaries in the classroom?
    c. Do I recognize the difference between showing emotion and attacking others?
    d. Do I have a plan for disrupting a bias incident?
    e. Do I understand the difference between neutrality and fairness?
    f. Have I practiced calling in?
6. Understanding student perceptions[3]
    a. Have I considered how imposter syndrome affects some students?
    b. Am I open to considering how students' experiences on and off campus affect their engagement in class?
    c. Do I think of the student body as a monolith, or recognize differences in their readiness to engage with me and with each other?
    d. Am I able to recognize what is happening in a quiet classroom?
    e. Is my classroom environment intimidating?
    f. Am I certain all students feel equally heard in my classroom?

3. Remarks by Chanelle Bonsu, "The Quiet Classroom."

INDEX